Little People's Mental Health: Easy, Manageable, Guidance

Suitable for ALL Parents with a Child of Primary School Age

First published in Great Britain in 2020

The Author and Editor have made every effort to ensure that the websites and statistics cited within this book were up to date and correct at the time of going to press. The Author and Editor are not responsible for the continued accessibility, content, or quality of such websites.

Paperback ISBN: 978-1-8380965-0-2

E-Book ISBN: 978-1-8380965-1-9

About the Author

Tammy Fioravanti-Clarkson, BSc Hons Psychology, PgDip Couns, MBACP, is a British Author and practising Children's Therapist, currently working in her own independent practice in London.

She has worked with children for nearly two decades, in a range of settings, including nurseries, schools, family homes and clinical environments.

Tammy currently works Therapeutically with families, supporting children and teenagers displaying general mental health difficulties, including those with highly complex needs and disorders.

In 2018, Tammy was awarded 'Best Mental Health Professional' by GHP Private Healthcare Awards and achieved the notable 2018 'Woman of the Future UK' Award for her work in setting up a Children's Wellness Centre. Her independent mental health practice won the 2020 West London 'Health and Well-Being' Award.

Little People's Mental Health: Easy, Manageable, Guidance
Edited By: Pamela Bentley

For my husband and daughter

Little People's Mental Health: Easy, Manageable, Guidance

Tammy Fioravanti-Clarkson

Chapters

Preface

If you are a parent with a child between the age of 4 - 11 years, then my aim is that this book will be of great use to you, throughout their entire primary school journey. The concept behind it, is that a child does not have to be in need of support, for parents to strive to sustain and enhance their emotional well-being.

Mental health does not just have to be in decline for us to focus on *maintaining* and *improving* it.

This book will encompass an array of topics that I can guarantee almost every parent with a child of primary school age will encounter at some point. Many of the chapters will cover ongoing issues that are likely to be common occurrences, appearing throughout your child's school life. By equipping parents with the skills and knowledge, long-term positive mental health can be promoted within the home environment, resulting in the reduction of the number of children in need of Therapeutic support.

Parents can play a fundamental role in supporting their child's mental health and with practise can achieve, *at home*, some of the core goals that external Therapy sessions aim to bring about.

If you are currently worried about your child's mental health, then this book will provide ideas and techniques that you can implement at home, to enhance their overall well-being and hopefully prevent difficulties from escalating further.

After years of working with children and families in school, home, educational and clinical settings, I have seen repetitive, common mental health trends that surface throughout early childhood. The examples and case studies in this book, which will most likely resonate with many parents, are fictionalised, however, all stem from multiple real-life situations that I have observed repeatedly over the years. This book will *not* discuss complex research studies that are written in a way that is impossible to understand, but instead will include easy, manageable, guidance that is simple to follow.

Although I have worked with children in extreme distress, due to marital breakdown, violence, abuse, neglect and trauma, including children self-harming and suicidal, this book does not focus on severe mental health concerns. Instead, it will explore mental health holistically and how our general home life can fundamentally influence a child's overall well-being and their future.

One thing I think is important to note, is that this book is suitable for *any* parent with a child of primary school age. I strongly believe and have seen first-hand that mental health difficulties can affect anyone, regardless of class or culture. I have worked with children whose families are on zero / low incomes and on state benefits, to those who live in highly affluent geographical areas. My work has allowed me to support children in nurseries and underprivileged state schools, through to children attending private schools, including the most prestigious and sought-after public schools in the UK. Yet, what I have observed, is that although the initial rationale behind a child coming to see me may vary greatly, the residing mental health effects of anxiety, stress and changes in behaviour are so similar in so many children. Mental health issues have no barriers - they are not defined by class or money. Just like a common cold, any single person, regardless of their background, can be impacted.

As a result, the similarities regarding mental health 'symptoms' in children under the age of 11 years, have led me to create this book, in order to give parents an extra helping hand. It will include simple tips and ideas to initiate at home, to maintain and improve a child's overall mental health.

CHAPTER ONE

Introduction to Children's Mental Health

Why support our children's mental health?

As an Integrative Children's Therapist, from my experience, children only ever come to see me when their mental health is in decline and they need some support to 'boost' this. In contrast, in other countries and cultures, sometimes Therapy is actually initiated not because of a negative experience or a decline in mental health, but in order to simply *maintain* overall well-being. Perhaps, in an ideal world, children would see a Therapist once a week, in order to promote a sense of self-maintenance around their mental health; just as they may attend a weekly sport or exercise activity to support their physical health. If this *were* in place, society may be very different and the ever-growing statistics around childhood mental health difficulties could be reduced. However, we must be realistic and not idealistic and quite simply, weekly Therapy for every child in the country is not something that is practical or manageable, and, like the majority of other health services, we only tend to seek these out when in need.

When we think of the word 'healthy' we can categorise this in terms of physical health, mental health, social well-being and the absence of disease or long-term illness. In order to enhance our immune system and physical health, there are a variety of things that we can strive to do, in terms of our diet, physical fitness, medication and general self-care. Therefore, taking into consideration how we may support our physical health and strengthen our immune system, it is equally important to consider mental health, especially for our children, in the same way.

We must support our children in feeling emotionally healthy to cope with the demands of life, regardless of whether or not we currently have concerns about their overall mental health.

For ease, (although mental health would not be assessed in this way), let us try and envision children's mental health simplified as a scale, via the following diagram.

Image One:

C-----------------------------------**B**-----------------------------------**A**

Intervention Required | General Well-Being | High Emotional Health

C = Intervention Required:
A child may be struggling with their behaviour, emotions or self-esteem, as a result of several different factors or experiences. This feeling of poor mental health is likely to be present over a long period of time, with the child finding it difficult to bounce back from difficulties. It is likely that they will need some external support from a trained professional.

B = General Well-Being:
A child can generally manage their home and school life positively, with no external professional help required. They may have episodical difficulties from time to time, but can usually cope with these via support from the adults around them.

A = High Emotional Health:
A child appears resilient, self-assured and confident, able to cope well with the demands of life. They demonstrate positivity towards themselves, have healthy relationships with those around them and can manage an array of feelings, from sadness to anger, bouncing back from tougher times and challenging situations.

Let us imagine that point B is where most children, who are not in need of, or who are not seeking external mental health support, may sit. The majority of children that I work with come to see me because they are currently starting to fall below this imaginary well-being rating of B. They are experiencing difficulties that are causing them to enter point C, when external professional mental health intervention is required.

I am the biggest advocate of children's Therapy and have seen first-hand the unbelievable benefits this can have on a child's well-being and will always encourage families to seek support in times of need - the final chapter in this book will discuss exactly how to find a Therapist and what to expect from a children's Therapeutic service. Yet, in many cases, I also have observed that there are *so many things* that parents can do at home which can help improve a child's mental health, in a similar way that regular Therapy sessions strive to achieve.

What if parents can promote such positive mental health and resilience at home, that their child on an average day-to-day basis could feel so emotionally healthy, that on many days they feel at point A?

Perhaps that means when faced with challenges and difficulties that every family will endure, children who have developed these positive coping skills and resilience during their primary school years, via their home life and parental influence, hopefully will not slip down all the way to point C, when things are challenging. This book is about just that; encouraging ways that parents can *develop* and *maintain* positive mental health at home and so attain the core goals that Therapeutic intervention aims to bring about – *without needing to see a Therapist.*

Part of the rationale behind this book, is to try and decrease the overwhelming number of children in the United Kingdom who are in need of mental health support, by providing parents with the ‘tools’ to bring about positive mental health within their home environment. Research in 2020, from The Place2Be (The UK’s leading Mental Health Children’s Charity) reported that 1 in every 8 children have a diagnosable mental health condition. Fifty percent of those with lifetime mental health problems first experienced symptoms *before* the age of 14 years. In a standard state school classroom, this averages that around 3 children in every single class may be suffering greatly from poor mental health. It is important to consider that these statistics are based on ‘diagnosable conditions’ such as Depression, Bi-Polar Disorder, Generalised Anxiety Disorder, Attention Deficit Hyperactivity Disorder, Social Anxiety and Personality Disorder. On average, ninety percent of the children and young people I work with do not have any form of ‘diagnosable’ condition whatsoever, yet would still be classed as having moderate, to severe mental health difficulties. They would not likely be classified within this range of statistics, thus meaning the number of children struggling with their mental health is in fact far more than we could ever account for.

The statistics are astounding and troubling and only appear to be increasing, in our ever-changing society, where pressures on both parents and children can feel overwhelming and intense. Although mental health support for children is accessible on the NHS, the unbelievable demand means a child can wait well over a year to receive any form of treatment, which in some cases, can result in further mental health decline. It can be a tumultuous task for parents to access this kind of support, with of course many families in no position to seek private help due to the high costs.

We *can* decrease this by offering further support and education around childhood mental health to parents, who after all, are their child's first and most important educators!

Although there are many aspects of a child's life that are beyond a parents' control, one thing that every parent can strive to regulate as much as possible, is their child's home life. I strongly believe that armed with the right knowledge and understanding, parents can create an atmosphere at home that supports a child's positive sense of mental health, aiming to build resilient, confident, self-aware, open, and emotionally mature children. These children are likely to be more equipped to deal with what life may throw at them and the pressures and demands that secondary school will inevitably bring about. This book demonstrates ways of creating, establishing and maintaining a sense of overall mental health well-being; just in the same way we may strive to give our child balanced meals, or vitamin supplements in order to fend off any nasty bugs or infections. Mental health can be viewed in the same way, and, as parents you can be instrumental in helping to stop these difficulties in their tracks before they escalate.

As you progress through the book, you will notice that each chapter initially lists 'Therapeutic Goals' in order to bring about increased positive mental health. These are the 'goals' that would be focused on should you seek external help for your child and are listed within each chapter because I *strongly* believe they can also be supported by parents *at home.*

At the end of the book, you will see a 'Notes' section, whereby you can jot down anything that resonates highly with you, or you would like to refer back to at a later date.

CHAPTER TWO

Expressing Feelings and Emotions

Therapeutic Goals to be considered at home:

· Helping children to accept and understand that it is natural to experience a range of different feelings and emotions every day

· Helping children to develop a thorough emotional vocabulary, naming out loud how they feel, thus increasing their own self-awareness

· Helping children to express and share both positive and negative feelings, in appropriate, safe, and healthy ways

How this builds Positive Mental Health:

· Helps a child feel secure in managing and coping with many different feelings and emotions

· Ensures a child feels understood by those around them, reducing inappropriate behaviours and helping them to learn more about who they are as a person

· Encourages a child to develop healthy behavioural patterns, preventing confusing emotions being expressed in potentially dangerous ways, such as self-harm

Why are feelings and emotions so important?

This chapter will discuss ways children may express their emotions and feelings and how internal confusion can sometimes lead to disruptive, unsafe, or inappropriate behaviour. We will examine why it is fundamentally so important for children to develop an emotional vocabulary and increased self-awareness, whilst exploring the essential role parents can play in this at home - without the need for Therapeutic intervention.

One of the key goals of Therapy with a child is to help them to understand and learn more about their feelings and emotions. It may sound simple, but actually for many children understanding the unsettling world of their emotions can be a momentous task, causing huge behavioural responses. Most children are likely to understand 'happy' and 'sad' reactions, yet there are so many other emotions caught up between these positive and negative feelings, for example, envy, jealousy, rage, anger, frustration, excitement, optimism, disappointment etc. Trying to understand these significant thoughts, can be unbelievably confusing for many primary school aged children. Considering feelings rarely remain stagnant, it is important to remember that children are trying to adapt and learn about something which is constantly changing, depending on their experiences. It is therefore understandable why children may, at times, feel confused and express their feelings and emotions in inappropriate or negative ways. This is not only frustrating for children and parents, but can have long-term detrimental effects on mental health, which will be demonstrated within this chapter.

Developmental emotional changes throughout the early years

Emotional expression is innate from birth; although for many new sleep-deprived parents, it can sometimes feel like their baby is screaming purely to test them - although it is important to hold onto the fact that babies only cry as a way of communicating a need. Through careful parenting and striving to understand what these different communication cues mean, via trial and error, parents can learn to respond to these distinct cries to meet their baby's needs. As babies grow and develop, their expressions of emotions begin to not only represent their needs, but their wants and desires too. Toddlers are likely to scream or cry if they see a toy which is unattainable. Although this emotional expression may feel just attention-based, it is due to a lack of developmental understanding from that child. They can see the toy, so why can they not have it? Toddlerhood is commonly referred to as the 'Terrible Twos' with this fundamental period of growth and development, often resulting in parents feeling like they are on a constant roundabout of not quite knowing when the next meltdown will occur! Part of parenthood in the early years is likely to be a guessing game and parents have an incredibly hard job navigating the first few years with an irrational little person, who is yet to develop the brain capacity to understand that you are trying to help!

Responding to children's emotional expressions is probably one of the greatest challenges of parenting, usually more apparent in the early years, then resurfacing again with brain changes throughout adolescence. Even if these emotional expressions occur within the expectations of children's developmental stages, they can still be fundamentally difficult to predict, prevent and understand. Many parents say that they feel their child has not grown out of the 'Terrible Twos' and that the emotional expressions their child is still displaying is beyond what they think is 'normal'. Although developmentally, by the time a child reaches primary school age, these outbursts should have subsided, it can be common for tantrums and meltdowns to continue occurring in these particular school years.

Perhaps we can view childhood a little like a sandwich; we have the early years and the adolescent years as the bread enveloping the filling inside - the primary school years. The years when your child should be rational enough to not explode like a toddler, and rational enough to not explode like a teenager! However, for many sandwiches, the filling is often the most crucial part and the primary school years should be seen in just this way - these vital years help to educate, shape and mould your child into the person they are, helping them to become self-aware and resilient, ready to face the next layer of bread - the teenage times. Our goal is to equip children throughout these fundamental years to feel emotionally healthy.

As children get older, their thoughts and feelings become more complex, stemming from growing experiences and increased pressures and demands. Becoming emotionally healthy is not something that we simply achieve overnight, but is something that is ongoing throughout childhood; just in the same way one week of healthy meals does not make a child's immune system permanently strong. Given that feelings are present daily, for all of humankind, it is important we are continually supporting our children with their understanding as they mature.

Nowadays, many children are becoming hormonal and entering puberty well before they even begin secondary school. A child with an increasing understanding of their emotions and feelings is likely to be better equipped to deal with these changes, especially if they have an open home environment, where verbalisation is respected and encouraged.

Habitual responses to feelings

As your child navigates their way through primary school, new experiences will naturally bring about new feelings and emotions which are not always easy for them to comprehend. When emotions, feelings, and bodily responses to feelings, are not fully understood by a child, this can result in frustration and cause upset which is likely to then be expressed behaviourally. These behaviours can become habitual and consequently be repeated over and over again.

The following examples are situations where a certain misunderstood feeling has caused a habitual behavioural pattern to develop.

1. Rosy struggles with maths = Rosy feels frustrated and stupid = Rosy refuses to do maths = when mum / dad says it is homework time, Rosy starts shouting and will not do any work = Rosy gets into trouble at home and at school = Rosy starts to struggle with any expectations placed on her.

Rosy has developed an association with feeling inadequate when she does her work. Her shouting at mum / dad is an expression of her inner turmoil. Over months, this develops into Rosy shouting at her parents every time they, or a teacher requests something of her; even though it may not always be homework related.

2. Logan feels jealous when mum / dad picks up his baby brother = Logan hits baby brother and also mum / dad = Logan is put in time-out = Logan feels even more angry = Logan now hits baby brother every time he is holding something that belongs to him.

Logan has developed an association between feeling jealous and his baby brother. He uses his fists to express his inner feelings. Even if Logan does not actually want the toy his baby brother is holding, his jealousy will surface, reminding him of previous negative feelings, and he will hit the baby regardless.

3. Annie felt nervous and had a funny feeling in her tummy when trying out a new after-school club; so much so that she started crying in front of all the other girls = Annie ran out of the room and mum / dad had to come back and collect her = every time Annie now feels nervous, or her tummy feels like it has butterflies, she runs away from the situation.

Annie has developed an association between feeling nerves and taking herself away from the situation as fast as she can. Annie does not understand what is happening in her tummy, so every time she feels nervous, her immediate reaction is to get into 'flight' mode.

The previous examples discuss frustration, feelings of inadequacy, jealousy, and nervousness; all feelings that are highly common for children in primary school to experience. Rosy, Logan and Annie did not understand what they were feeling and experiencing and just understood it as 'bad' and 'negative.' In these situations, it is so easy for any child to associate the confusing feelings they felt in the past, with new experiences, causing the habitual behavioural patterns to surface. This can make it appear like a child is presenting with challenging behaviours, in multiple different areas of their life.

When there is a habitual behavioural pattern, it is natural as parents to immediately attend to the behaviours first. Of course, the actions of Rosy, Logan and Annie need to be addressed, however, sometimes tackling the displayed behaviour can take all our focus and energy. This means we are often not considering the *reason* and the *communication* of emotion behind these behaviours, especially if our child is not expressing to us how they *really* feel. It may sound complex, but this chapter will shortly explore how we can try and understand the hidden feelings beneath our children's responses. We need to also help our children identify them. This is essential in helping them become emotionally healthy and resilient.

Behaviour is always a communication of a feeling - no child randomly behaves in a specific way; there is always a reason behind it. However, uncovering this feeling and communication may feel like detective work. Hopefully, the further we progress through this chapter, the easier this will feel to achieve.

Feelings and behavioural responses

The next two case studies demonstrate even further how easy it is for a child's behaviour to become the main focus, when really, what was needed was support with their hidden, underlying feelings.

Case Study: Coco aged 5

Everyone around her thought Coco may have ADHD, (Attention Deficit Hyperactivity Disorder) when in fact Coco's behaviour was purely an expression of her anxiety. When Coco felt nervous, or worried, she would feel her heart racing and her tummy felt funny. Coco did not know what this meant, and this scared her. This worry then came out in hyperactive physical behaviour, as Coco tried to combat the strange (but totally natural) physical symptoms she was experiencing.

Case Study: Larry aged 8

Larry had seen something worrying on the news about a child dying after eating grapes and subsequently could not get it out of his head. Not wishing to look 'silly' he did not talk about it. When chewing, he felt his throat constricting and his heart beating fast, meaning his eating habits completely changed. Larry could not express this great internal anxiety, which resulted in an escalating negative pattern of behaviour. He would start to shout and get angry at mealtimes, pushing his food away. His parents, unaware of his anxiety, naturally focused on his inappropriate behaviour.

Larry did not understand this deep anxiety he was feeling. He had heard of 'worry' and had spoken to his parents many times about this, in terms of worrying about not getting his homework done on time etc - but this felt different. Often anxiety differs from worry as it tends to include more bodily symptoms and can be felt far more strongly. Larry physically felt this anxiety in his throat and his chest when he was about to eat - hence causing him to feel hesitant around food.

The hyperactivity of Coco and the shouting and aggression of Larry became the main focus, however what both children needed was actually quite similar - they simply needed some understanding about what was happening in their bodies, causing them to feel certain ways.

Physical feelings / sensations

As adults, we can all probably identify certain physical feelings we have felt within our bodies, which were responses to specific experiences. There are times we may sweat when nervous, feel the need to expel energy by pacing a room when waiting for news, feel our heart beating faster when excited or angry, feel our breath increasing when annoyed, or feel our face turning red when embarrassed or awkward. As much as these bodily reactions can be frustrating and often beyond our control, we usually understand them and why they are there.

However, imagine experiencing some of these symptoms, or many of them all at once, and having no clue whatsoever what is happening to your body and brain - I am sure many of us would be reaching for our phone, or even rushing to A&E! The first experience of a panic attack has in fact sent many people to hospital, in the fear that they were having a heart attack or another medical emergency - the main reason being, they were experiencing the unknown. Imagine how scary and bewildering it can be for our children then.

It is imperative to educate children on their bodily responses, by letting them know that they are OK and that you sometimes feel that way too. Do not 'assume' your child is having a certain physical response. Try to observe what you see and hear them tell you. Talking about other physical responses they may indeed *not* be experiencing will only confuse and worry them.

Of course, it is about finding your own words and ways to talk to your child, but here are a few ideas:

"Right here in our chest is our heart... sometimes it might feel like it is going really fast if we are feeling..."

"Some people think it feels like a really big drum in their chest when they feel ..."

"I have noticed that you are breathing really fast right now. Maybe that is because you are upset. Sometimes we might breathe extra fast after we have just had a big cry"

"Sometimes when people try something new for the first time, they get a funny feeling in their tummy"

"Perhaps it might feel a bit like your tummy is spinning like a washing machine, or like a butterfly is fluttering around. Don't worry there is nothing like that in your tummy! It is just your body letting you know that you are feeling a little nervous, or worried"

"It is OK if sometimes we might feel really hot and a little sweaty when we feel ... I wonder if that is how you might be feeling right now?"

Educating and supporting children in understanding this, is a step forward in helping them develop self-awareness, whilst also helping their resilience to develop in terms of managing their emotions. Teach them that these physical feelings will come and go in different situations, but that they will also always fade. For some older children, it may also help them to understand that we experience these sensations, because when we feel a certain way, our brain communicates with our body, which then releases a special chemical - known as a hormone or neurotransmitter. These special chemicals make us feel certain ways. It might sound beyond your child's maturity to share facts like this with them, but often clear explanations can help reduce worry.

Lack of understanding around feelings

Inappropriate behaviour can also come about, not just due to a lack of understanding of bodily sensations, but also due to a general lack of awareness around different, everyday feelings.

Often a child displaying undesirable behaviour is responding to a feeling that they either do not like, or do not understand. I am sure every parent can think of situations when they may have said "no" to their child, which resulted in a huge outburst. Although this is developmentally common, sometimes this goes beyond just not getting what they want. Often those confusing feelings of jealousy, envy, disappointment, and unfairness that come with hearing "no" can feel overwhelming and confusing for a child.

At times, it is not always the limit imposed or the word "no" that causes an upset, but the confusing accompanying feelings that come with it. This is explored more with the case study of Tom.

Case Study: Tom aged 6

Tom would have huge tantrums everyday if he did not get what he wanted, or if mum / dad asked something of him. Tom would hit, shout, stamp his feet, scream, and even bite his parents, causing great conflict at home.

Tom quite simply just needed help to understand his feelings and emotions. When demands were placed on him, or he did not get what he wanted, he experienced a stress-response and was unable to manage or appropriately express the accompanying feelings of upset, disappointment, annoyance, overwhelm and more. Unfortunately, Tom's behaviours had developed into a negative pattern and every time Tom felt a certain way (that he did not understand) he would routinely get into 'fight' mode and hit out. He had simply learnt to respond to his emotions in this way.

Naturally, this developed into a pattern of mum / dad becoming angry and frustrated and responding to the aggressive behaviour, causing Tom to lash out even more. A child who has constant regular tantrums often has not learnt appropriate ways to express their feelings, and as a result the build-up of stress-hormones causes meltdowns and their behaviour can appear aggressive.

I talk to many parents whose children come to Therapy because of behaviours such as aggression, hitting, rivalry, excessive tantrums, and defiance. On many occasions these behavioural concerns are often the result of a build-up, over time, of unprocessed emotions that a child cannot comprehend. The longer this goes on for, the harder it can be to tackle, because of learnt behavioural and thought patterns, and the external focus naturally being on the behaviour itself. In the case of Tom, he simply needed support in understanding different feelings, learning how to respond to them and learning that all the feelings he experienced were OK.

It is important to remember that at times, emotional outbursts and lack of understanding around feelings and thought processes, can be signs of more complex issues such as learning difficulties, or neurodevelopmental disorders, for example, ADHD (Attention Deficit Hyperactivity Disorder) or Autism. If you have concerns which you feel may be beyond the remit of this book, please do seek guidance, as the sooner a child is assessed, the more successful the intervention support can be.

The following key steps in emotional understanding around feelings and emotions were exactly what Tom needed, however these steps are important to consider for *every* child, when striving for positive mental health. Perhaps take a moment or use the 'Notes' section of the book to consider whether your child possesses this understanding. Ways to encourage this at home will then be explored.

Key steps in emotional understanding

1- Help a child to **acknowledge** that everyone has feelings, which we all experience daily

2- Help a child to **identify** what a specific feeling may be called

3- Help a child **understand** the effects these feelings may have on their body

4- Help a child to **associate** specific feelings and specific experiences; for example, visiting new places and feeling nervous

5- Help a child to **accept** that all feelings are OK, even negative feelings

6- Help a child **verbalise** what they are feeling to others

7- Help a child **express** the effects of their feelings in appropriate / safe ways

8- Help a child feel confident to **cope** should these feelings arise again

9- Help a child to identify how those around them may be feeling and ways to respond appropriately to **others' needs**.

Keeping in mind the 9 key steps, the following pages will provide some ideas and exercises that can be carried out at home. They will also offer thought provoking questions with regards to your own behaviours as parents. Sometimes altering our mindsets can be more fruitful in bringing about positive change than just a specific 'strategy'.

It is important to remember that every single child will experience an array of feelings and emotions every single day. Adding extra 'tools' to your child's emotional 'toolbox', whether you currently have any concerns, or not, is always going to be of benefit.

Our own behaviours and attitudes

First and foremost, in order to support our child in developing the key steps of emotional understanding, we need to take a little look at our own behaviours as parents and examine what messages they may be portraying to our children. It is natural to just want solutions and ideas based around our children themselves, but it is imperative to remember that for those in their primary school years, the majority of what they learn is observational, from the key adults in their life - their parents. Our own attitudes and behaviours are crucial in aiding their emotional development.

One of the main ways that we work through our 9 key steps, is through unconscious teaching i.e. letting our children learn through observing us.

Verbalising feelings and responding appropriately to feelings is imperative in raising emotionally healthy children, but... *do you do this as parents?*

We cannot expect our child to behave and respond to situations in certain ways if we do not mirror this ourselves. There are two important goals to consider in relation to our own actions, before moving on and supporting our children with their own.

1. Being more aware of your own feelings and emotions and the impact they have on your moods

When juggling the demands of life, it is common for any parent to say that they have had a 'bad' day. However, sometimes trying to narrow it down, as to exactly what caused this feeling can help.

Perhaps think of the last time you had a tough day at work or had a meeting that felt like it went terribly wrong, or a meal with a friend that left you feeling upset. Try and untangle your feelings further. Could it have been disappointment or jealousy / frustration at not having met expectations / anger directed at your boss for unfair treatment, or anxiety that hindered your performance in a meeting?

Understanding why the day was so bad, can mean that negativity will not keep repeating itself over and over. Find an explanation and a solution so that it does not happen again. A future strategy can massively help us turn a bad day into a positive one.

Like everything, we cannot teach our children skills to support themselves, if we do not do this ourselves.

2. Sharing out loud your feelings and emotions with your children

Often, we want to shield our feelings and emotions from our children to protect them, but it is actually far more positive for their own development, for them to see their mum / dad feeling a certain way. Not only does it teach children verbal understanding, but helps them to accept that emotions and feelings are a way of life, and not something to shy away from. It also demonstrates to a child, that mum / dad may have experienced a certain negative response, but they can cope with this, manage, and move on. This example demonstrates to children that *they* also have the strength within them to do the same.

Next time, if you have had a 'bad' day and your mood may be present for your child to see, explain to them why and how you feel, using descriptive emotive language - for example, "I feel... jealous, annoyed, disappointed, hurt, excited, frustrated, agitated..."

Your child may not need to know the ins and outs of exactly what happened, but they can understand a simple, "I feel really disappointed because I thought I had done well on something, but my boss says I need to do even more work!" Your child may know nothing about your job, but your sharing may resonate with them about something in their life - perhaps their teacher marked their homework poorly and they cried. Your use of the word 'disappointed', may help your child to understand that word, in accordance with their own life, a little more.

How about... "I'm just a little envious at the moment, as Susan has bought that brand-new coffee machine that I really wanted!" Your child may not care about coffee machines, but they can learn that it is acceptable to feel this way, if someone else has something that they may really want. Your child can also see that you are not running next door and taking Susan's coffee machine (!) allowing them to understand that we can all have feelings like this, but do not need to act on them.

Apologising to your child

Every adult and every child will, from time to time experience negative moods. As human beings it is natural that we occasionally take our feelings out on those around us. If your child reacted inappropriately, by lashing out or shouting at a family member after experiencing a 'bad' day themselves, would you ask them to apologise?

What would happen if you had a bad day yourself and ended up snapping unnecessarily at your child? Once calm, would you apologise to them?

Showing remorse or apologising to your children (in whatever way fits your family) is important. Saying sorry and explaining to your child exactly how you felt and why you may have behaved in a certain way can be incredibly cathartic, not only strengthening your relationship with your child (a key factor of positive mental health), but also teaches your child that difficult feelings, resulting in mistakes, are OK. You do not want your child to carry an internal guilt every time they do something wrong. This is likely to cause problems with self-esteem later. It is important for a child to know mum / dad can make mistakes and it is something that we all do. This can support children in learning to accept and move on from their *own* mistakes.

Once *you* feel confident in sharing and verbalising your own thoughts to your child, you can then start to feel more confident in helping them understand their own feelings.

Our children's feelings

To reiterate, in the case studies we explored earlier, the child's behaviour was a response to a feeling that they were unable to clearly communicate.

The next few paragraphs will explore how we can try and see through the expressed, presented behaviour, to help your child understand what they may be truly feeling.

Remember, all behaviour is a communication and your own use of words, expressions of emotion and verbalisation of feelings, can go a long way in educating your child and helping them become emotionally healthy.

Let us think about some examples of common, everyday family conflict that you may have experienced. We will then explore some possible responses and techniques to similar situations.

1. A lovely family time playing a board game, until your child gets irritable, loses the game, perhaps is egged on by a sibling… the board gets tipped upside down, pieces are everywhere, and a beautiful picture-

perfect scene has turned into chaos, with your child screaming and crying.

2. Homework - the dreaded H word! Perhaps it is a constant battle - maybe you are being screamed at that you are doing it wrong. Your child cannot do it either. Maybe you start to bribe them. Maybe the homework gets thrown on the ground!

3. Dinner time - a wonderful opportunity for calm family time, but in the real world this often becomes a perfect opportunity for arguments to begin. Apparently, your child hates sausages, when yesterday they loved them... their brother has more chips on their plate than they do... the shouting and face-pulling starts!

In all these circumstances, the immediate behaviour *does* need to be addressed if aspects of safety come into play, especially if another child has been hit or hurt in the process, or something has been thrown and glass is on the floor.

However, if there are no safety concerns involved, it can be useful to engage in something I call the **PERT** technique, next time there is commotion in your household.

· **Pause**

· **Evaluate**

· **Reflect**

· **Touch**

Give yourself a moment to **pause**, before saying the first words that come into your mind. Pausing will also help your own mental state. Behavioural responses can often be contagious - we see someone angry with us and our mood state can suddenly change dramatically. If your child is screaming and shouting at you, it is often natural to respond back in a similar fashion, but I am sure you will agree, it probably does not help the situation – hence, the importance of taking a few seconds to pause. This will give you time to think a little more clearly and calmly. Some people like to count to a certain number before reacting, others may recite the alphabet quickly in their head. Another good idea is to breathe in for 5 seconds, hold for 2 seconds and breathe out for 6 seconds.

While pausing, **evaluate** the situation briefly, to understand what has happened, and hopefully why.

Immediate response: (without pausing) That is not OK! Why did you do that? Get off your brother! Go to your room! Pick up the pieces! The game is ruined! Why is family time always like this? No screen time for a week!

Evaluative response: (with pausing) My child must be unbelievably overwhelmed to have behaved in this way. What triggered this disruptive behaviour? Maybe something happened at school today? I can see how hard my child tried and they still lost the game. I am in control of this situation now and I am the adult. Let me calm the situation down and then talk about it.

Reflect on what you think just happened, using words that may resonate with how your child may be feeling. Remember do not assume, but get used to using words such as - perhaps, maybe, I think, I wonder...

For example – "maybe you are frustrated" / "perhaps you are annoyed right now" / "I can understand you might be feeling a little worried" / "it can feel disappointing to lose a game"

This reflecting not only helps to educate a child around the verbalisation of feelings and emotions, but the sense of being overwhelmed lessens, when there is an *actual* word for how they are feeling. It also helps a child feel understood and heard, which may decrease the inappropriate behaviour.

Touch / comfort: In situations like these, often what a child needs is some form of comfort, or touch, or a hug. Biologically, experiencing a hug or touch from someone you love releases a hormone called 'oxytocin', which can help us to feel more relaxed. Sometimes just gently holding your child's arms or offering a loving stroke can offer them a feeling of being 'contained' - thus helping them contain their own emotions too.

I can completely understand that in situations where a child has acted inappropriately, a hug may feel unsuitable - is it rewarding the behaviour? Is it teaching a child that it is OK to act like that? You can make your decision on this, dependent on what has happened, but for some children it is just what they need to help them calm down, reach a rational level of thinking and stop further escalation of behaviour.

Of course, inappropriate behaviour must be dealt with, but the *timing* of when it is dealt with is imperative. If you are trying to impose consequences on a child who is overwhelmed and in a heightened state of alert, it is not likely to have much of an impact. The general rule of thumb is that you need to help get your child from level 10, back down a few levels, before trying to educate them on the rights and wrongs of how they just behaved.

It may be common in your family to send your child to their room, or have time-out as a consequence, and if that is how you discipline in your home, ensure your child is on the verge of calming down *first*. Sending a child away who is completely overwhelmed and emotional is likely to make matters worse and make the entire scenario last longer. It is actually sending the message to a child that emotions are not OK, and they must be sent away the moment they react - this is not helpful for overall mental health long-term.

After engaging in PERT, then is the time to decide how you as a family operate - often some space is needed - perhaps a few moments alone to calm down may be what your child needs. Only once your child is completely calm, should you discuss their behaviour with them. Be sure to be clear it is their *behaviour*, and not *them* that was inappropriate and if need be, then impose your consequences.

I can almost guarantee, if you shout out "no screen time tonight," immediately after the behavioural episode, or whilst your child is currently having a tantrum, you will gain nothing. Further hysteria and upset will build as your child attempts to contemplate and process both the initial upset and now the imposed consequence too. This can have an immediate, short-term negative impact on a child's mental health as well as the potential long-term negative impact, if this is a pattern that ensues every time your child displays inappropriate behaviour.

Wait until your child is calmer, then decide your family's next steps, for example, does my child need a few moments in time-out / alone? When totally calm, even if that is an hour later, discuss with your child why the *behaviour* was not appropriate and any consequences that you may have decided.

Finally, make sure that you move on - do not hold grudges, do not keep bringing up the situation after it has been dealt with. Let your child move on too and try to enjoy the rest of your day together.

Phrases to consider avoiding

Although the following phrases are commonly used, you may like to try to avoid using sentences like these in the future.

"Stop being angry!"

Anger is a natural feeling and we all experience it. No one can just stop being angry and sometimes anger can help us as a form of release. It is important to teach children that **all** feelings are OK, even negative ones, like anger. What is not OK, is acting inappropriately to anger. This is important and applies for all 'negative' emotions.

"Why are you so angry?" / "Why are you being unreasonable?" / "Why did you throw the game?" / "Why didn't you listen?"

In a state of emotional upset, your child is overwhelmed and will most probably not be able to answer any of these questions rationally or sensibly. It is in fact putting extra stress on them to think of how to word the correct answer to you. They may not have even thought it properly through themselves, or even fully understood why they actually behaved like that yet. Perhaps try to avoid the use of the word 'why'.

"You must be so happy your friend is back from their trip!"

Remember as the adult it is your role to help your child decipher feelings, but we cannot predict what exactly is going on in their minds. Using phrases like 'should be' and 'must be' can be confusing for a child. If a child then thinks they should be feeling that way, when they do not, this can lead to a whole jumble of emotions that they cannot express.

"I am really disappointed in you"

The use of the 'feeling' word is positive, but make sure these words always describe the behaviour, never the child. "I am really disappointed in that behaviour" would be a far more suitable phrase - remember a child's sense of self is fragile and developing throughout primary school.

Parenting does not come with a script and it is not about learning unnatural ways to respond - of course, react and use appropriate phrases that feel natural to *you,* but consider the consequences certain wording may have.

Empathising with the feelings of others

We cannot control the peers that our children mix with, and unfortunately most children will meet and experience interactions with others who may not treat them well or who behave unkindly. Often children take this as a personal attack on them and over time, repeated negative behaviours from others can begin to affect a child's sense of self, and self-esteem. However, the more aware and emotionally healthy a child feels, the more they can distinguish others' feelings and behaviours, which are personal to that person, and nothing to do with themselves. Even for us as adults this is hard; it is natural for us to take negative behaviours, perhaps from our boss, as a personal assault, however more often than not, the behaviours we see from others, are due to their own personal circumstances and little to do with us. If we can equip our children with this understanding, it will take them far.

'Empathy' and 'sympathy', although they may sound very similar, are two very different things. Sympathy is showing and feeling compassion, or sorrow for someone else, whereas empathy is learning how to put yourself in the shoes of others, striving to understand what they may be experiencing and feeling. Children tend to start to develop empathy in their pre-school years, although some children are still developing it during primary school. As a result, it can be quite a task getting young children to share, as they simply do not have the brain capacity to understand viewpoints from the perspective of others.

Developing empathy, and understanding the feelings of others, can be important for children's overall mental health. It can help them develop long lasting, secure friendships with peers, encourages tolerance, acceptance and overall is the foundation of all human interactions. It is important to always encourage this in children from a young age and to contribute to this empathetic development, there are a few pointers you may like to consider.

1. If you are out and about and see another child displaying emotion, use it as a learning opportunity to wonder with your child what may have happened or how that child may be feeling. It can help your child build-on and practise their emotional vocabulary too.

2. If your child comes home from school, perhaps sharing some negative views towards other children in their class, try to help them look at it from the

perspective of that child too (whilst still of course validating how your child is feeling).

3. Use opportunities when another child may have been unkind to your child; help them understand why that child may have acted in a particular way. This will help them to realise it was not a personal attack on them, but that maybe the child was trying to manage their own feelings and were confused.

4. Bear in mind how much your child hears you moan about others. If you need to (and sometimes everyone does!) try and add some reflection about what the other person might be experiencing, causing him / her to act in that way.

Games and activities

Although striving for positive mental health is often not always about 'strategies' and 'methods', here are some ideas for those who may want more practical solutions to support the expression of feelings and emotional development within their child. It is important to note that positive mental health will not come about *just* from engaging in activities like these, and all the previous ideas within this chapter are still very important to consider incorporating within your home environment.

The feeling LEGO® game

1. Put a selection of LEGO® bricks in a box / hat / bag.

2. Create a colour-code key on a piece of paper whereby each colour relates to a certain feeling, for example RED - angry / BLUE - sad / GREEN - calm.

With older children, use several different colours and feelings. If you run out of colours and want to be inventive, put in some other random LEGO® pieces, for example, doors and windows and let them represent a different feeling too.

3. Be sure there is a mixture of positive feelings and negative feelings. Positive feelings help make the game a little more light-hearted and can allow for some funny stories too! Sit together as a family and clearly explain the rules first. Be clear about turn taking and listening to each other, to avoid conflict.

4. Take it in turns one at a time to pull out a brick and see on the key what it represents. That person must then share a time when they felt that way. Everyone else must listen.

How this activity supports mental health

· Adults need to engage in the game and share their experiences too – this helps children to *accept* and *understand* that all feelings are OK, especially if mum / dad have them too.

· It provides opportunities for children to share their own feelings in a way that feels informal and relaxed.

· It provides invaluable listening opportunities and insight into your child's inner world - try to avoid asking too many questions... let them share and then move on.

· It provides opportunities for family enjoyment and laughter (ideally try and share some funny stories yourself too).

· This game involves no winning or losing.

If you have a LEGO® base, each time you could place the brick on the base - who knows what random creation or model you will end up with!

JENGA® / brick game

If you liked the idea of the LEGO® game, it can also be played with JENGA®/ building bricks. You would need to write on the inside of each brick a different feeling (so you may want to have a spare JENGA® set).

Each time a player pulls out a piece they read the word and then share a memory in relation to that feeling.

This game may be more appropriate for older children who want a little more of a thrill, rather than just picking bricks out of a hat.

To avoid conflict / stress and a feeling of loss, if and when the tower falls, perhaps have a little bowl of funny forfeits - whoever causes the tower to fall picks one out at random. The forfeits are about having a laugh as a family, and not seeing the game as a winning opportunity.

Board games in general

As much as it can be natural to sometimes avoid these as a family in order to avoid conflict, they can offer invaluable opportunities for your child to feel different emotions and deal with them in a secure environment. Competitiveness, drama, winning and losing can all evoke a variety of feelings, such as excitement, suspense, frustration, jealousy, disappointment and more! These are all so useful for children to experience and understand for their present and future mental health and also offer you as parents the perfect opportunity to provide descriptive language, developing your child's emotional vocabulary.

Glitter jar

1. Find an old water bottle - ideally plastic.

2. Buy a small selection of coloured glitter and place them in bowls with a small spoon in each.

3. Sit down with your child and explain to them that each colour of glitter represents a feeling - let them decide which

colour represents what. Ideally the more feelings included the better. Alternatively, you could use small pom-poms or other coloured resources that can fit into a bottle neck.

4. Pour water into the bottle (about half full).

5. Let your child put a spoonful of every colour into the bottle, discussing the feeling each one represents. Pause and let them observe the glitter floating about. This activity can get a little messy; you may want to use a funnel.

6. After all the colours are in the bottle, screw the cap on tight!

7. Shake the bottle and observe all the colours mixing and floating within the water.

8. Explain to your child that this is a little like our feelings when we are overwhelmed.

9. Watch the glitter all sink back down to the bottom of the bottle and explain to your child, that even if things all feel confusing and muddled up sometimes, things always do calm down and settle again - just like the glitter in the jar.

Obviously your child can shake their bottle any time they need to, but it is useful to use this bottle again in moments of commotion and upset to help your child have a focus and remind themselves, that just like the mixed up glitter, they too will feel calm again soon.

In summary, feelings and emotions play a fundamental role in mental health and affect every child and adult (and many animals too). Sometimes I think of Therapy as a little like cooking / baking... the Therapist is the chef, holding the pot and observing the child throwing in all sorts of confusing, and maybe difficult emotions (the ingredients).

The chef's job is to help the child understand how to use all these ingredients wisely and in the correct proportions in order to end up with a successful result.

Without a chef, to the children, it can all look confusing and dishearten them, sometimes causing them to give up trying or display frustration because they 'just don't get it'. All they need is some help and guidance to produce something that makes them feel good.

Children in primary school often do not have the emotional maturity to be able to understand certain feelings and emotions and they often need adult help (i.e. the chef).

However, a child does not necessarily need a Therapist for this to happen. With the right 'tools', as a parent, you too can be their 'chef' helping the concoction of ingredients turn into something which makes sense. By looking deeper into your child's behaviours, emotions, and feelings you can help them, with understanding and guidance to have a strong healthy mind and a greater knowledge and understanding of who they are as a person.

Key 'takeaways' from this chapter to support positive mental health:

- ✓ A child's lack of understanding around feelings and emotions can cause inappropriate thinking and behavioural habits to develop. Consider the use of the **PERT** technique to prevent this escalating
- ✓ Children need support and education with regards to bodily sensations associated with different feelings
- ✓ There are 9 key steps to support a child's emotional understanding and vocabulary
- ✓ It is useful for parents to consider their own feelings and the verbalisation of these to their child
- ✓ Consider limiting the use of certain phrases which can cause situations to escalate
- ✓ Support your child's empathetic development towards other peoples' feelings
- ✓ Consider the use of fun games and activities to increase awareness and verbalisation of feelings and emotions

CHAPTER THREE

Encouraging Open Communication

Therapeutic Goal to be considered at home:

· Encouraging children to openly share their experiences, thoughts, worries or concerns

How this builds Positive Mental Health:

· Helps a child process and understand their experiences and thoughts, preventing a build-up of unresolved concerns

A key aim of Therapy with a child of primary school age is to support them in communicating their thoughts, feelings, and experiences - essentially, their 'inner world.' With a very young child this may be all through play, or art and we may communicate together via puppets, or small world toys. With an older child, the sessions may be more direct, with the child actively and openly talking to me. It is up to the child how they choose to communicate and share their world with me, and my role as a Therapist is to work in whatever way they feel comfortable. This brings about positive change because the child is releasing inner thoughts, and often inner turmoil, allowing themselves opportunities to explore past and present experiences and thought processes.

If a child does not have opportunities to process certain experiences, thoughts or emotions, then this can, in time, negatively impact their emotional health, overall resilience, and ability to cope in times of strife. Little worries build, turning into greater worries, affecting multiple areas of a child's life.

This communication, however, is something that I do believe can be fostered not just in Therapeutic settings, but also in home environments, preventing children from 'bottling up' concerns and feelings and enabling them to process situations and experiences with trusted adults - their parents.

Of course, it is not often within a busy family life that it is possible to sit and focus intently on everything your child does or says, in the way an hour-long Therapy session would allow. Instead, this brief chapter, alongside the previous strategies discussed in our 'Expressing Feelings and Emotions' chapter, aims to provide simple, manageable ideas and ways that open communication can be introduced, established, and maintained, long-term at home.

It may be worth considering, how much open communication occurs in your home - is there time set aside to speak with your child about their day or things that may be bothering them?

Do you feel your child would come to you if they had a problem that they needed adult support with?

Let us first think about the way we respond as parents when our child communicates with us. There are three factors to consider.

- Listening to the 'smalls'

- Listening with our 'eyes'

-Listening 'actively' with our ears

Listening to the 'smalls' is fundamental to think about in relation to your home dynamic. Open communication develops, with how we respond and support our child, and via the impression we are relaying to them when they are talking to us about the 'smalls'. These 'smalls' are the minor, seemingly unimportant aspects of their inner mind, which as adults we may actually find quite boring! For example, it could be the excitement over a 'stick' or 'leaf', a particular TV character, or toy they desperately would like - essentially, the mundane aspects of everyday life, that do not really take much brain power, as an adult, to respond to.

I am sure there have been many of these scenarios, when you were busy cooking the dinner, or thinking about your work meeting the next day, and, although you may have politely responded to what your child was expressing, it is perhaps likely that your response was not quite as meaningful as it could have been. This is understandable - it can be hard to get too excited about a snail, or dirty stone that your child has excitedly brought in from the garden. Perhaps your first reaction might even be to get the muddy object out the house!

However, if we do not sufficiently listen to the 'smalls', then we need to consider why would our child ever come to us with the 'bigs' - the troubling, worrying aspects of their life. Over time, they may feel that they will not get the reaction they want and need, and therefore store up inner thoughts and feelings to the detriment of their mental health. In hectic lives, especially with younger children and other siblings too, it is naturally not always possible to intently focus on your child's every word and conversation. It can be helpful though, to strive to focus on at least one or two 'smalls' a day using the following guidance.

Listening with our 'eyes'

This may initially sound strange, but a child can feel 'unheard' when there is a lack of eye contact during a conversation, that to them, is important. We should try and consider how this 'looks' for your child, if whilst they are talking to you, your eyes are elsewhere, busy and focused on another task, or two, and not at all on your child.

Realistically, it is not possible to do this every time your child says something - but just consider and be aware of your eye contact and try, at times, to stop what you are doing, look at them and acknowledge the fact that you are listening fully and intently.

Listening 'actively' with our ears

Again, this may seem a little strange - we all listen with our ears, do we not? However, the important point here, is the word 'active.'

Active listening is a skill that takes some practise and involves fully concentrating on what is being said, rather than just passively 'hearing.' It involves listening with all our senses. Let us look at what this means.

Facial expressions: We have explored eye contact, but is our expression conveying that we are responding appropriately to what is being shared, or are we planning tomorrow's lunch in our mind? Non-verbal cues make up a fundamental part of communication and what we portray with our expressions and body language, plays a huge role in how much the speaker (our child) feels listened to and heard.

Body language: Is our body language showing an interest in what is being shared with us? Are we leaning in towards our child, or nodding, conveying that we are hearing what is being said?

Tone of voice: Does this convey interest, or does it sound like we are eager for the conversation to end? Are we using words and sounds to demonstrate recognition of what is being relayed?

In fact, listening is actually very difficult! It is natural for a human being's mind to wander and trying to stop that from happening involves the use of extra brain processing capacity. Adding stress and tiredness into play (two common aspects of parenting) reinforce that listening is not always an easy job. Yet listening can really impact emotional health.

All the prior points bring about a feeling of being 'heard' - the notion of being heard is so important to mental health. A child can feel validated and respected, thus helping to create a positive sense of self within. When someone feels fully listened to, they often leave the conversation feeling 'lifted' - being fully listened to also helps to develop and strengthen relationships, creating feelings of trust and security. Listening may appear to be minor, but in fact, it is the very opposite.

Active listening is a fundamental part of Therapy and is far easier for a Therapist to do, than a parent in a busy home environment. However, with awareness, knowledge and practise, parents can perfect this skill, thus greatly supporting their child's communication and their overall mental health.

Before we think about open communication with the 'bigs', let us just spend a moment exploring the communication in between - what I would call the 'middles'. These are the topics that have more impact on your child's life than their 'stick' or 'leaf' conversations, but not something that is deeply troubling them to the extent you need to intervene.

The 'middles'

It is natural to want to reassure your child that things will be fine, especially if you are confident from past experiences that the issue will be gone by tomorrow. However, sometimes in doing this, it can feel to a child that we may not be fully hearing them, or in fact unconsciously belittling what they have shared. Just simply telling them everything will be OK is sometimes not what a child wants to hear. Let them vent, offload, and share. Demonstrate clearly that you have heard them. Things that may seem still quite minor to us in an adult world, may temporarily feel quite a big deal to a child.

Saying to a child "things will be fine" does not actually install any coping methods for future use. Rather, spending a few moments, fully listening to your child, reflecting what they have said, acknowledging their feelings and emotions and, if need be, helping them to see things from a different point of view, can benefit their emotional health and support future open communication at home. Assist your child with helpful ideas, to encourage the notion of solution-finding skills.

The 'bigs'

Usually when a child comes to Therapy, it is because they have, or are experiencing something which to them feels 'big', for example long-term friendship difficulties, anxiety, negative occurrences and so on, that they need to share, understand, and process.

Monitoring your responses to the 'smalls' and the 'middles' will make it more likely that your child will come to you with the 'bigs' too. This means you will have the opportunity to support your child with these difficulties, before their mental health becomes too impacted. Your listening techniques and responses to these communications are vital here to allow your child to feel fully heard. No matter how open the communication is at home, sometimes with the 'bigs' it is harder for children to naturally bring up these feelings, or experiences. Hence it is up to you as parents, to consider ways that you can provide opportunities at home for these to be broached.

Some guidance follows as to how this could be achieved.

Remember, maintaining positive mental health is an on-going process and changes need to be permanent for them to be effective - not carried out just once or twice.

Creating times to talk

It is important to consider your own child's personality and when and how this would work best for them. For example, some children may not be very responsive immediately after school, but a couple of hours later are more communicative. Others may respond better after exercise or a sports club, when they have had a chance to physically let off some steam. Also consider your own plans and weekly routine too. You do not want to create a 'talking time' for your child, only to unconsciously convey that you are distracted, or need to be elsewhere.

- **Time before bed**

For some children having 15 / 20-minutes before bed each night, to chat to mum / dad about their day, or their plans for tomorrow can make a substantial difference to their stress levels. Minor experiences can build up during the day, that if not processed, can develop over time into larger stressors. This time to talk, can offer invaluable opportunities, not only to strengthen your bond with your child, but to encourage open communication and once again benefit their overall emotional health. Bear in mind that for an exhausted child, and an over-thinker, before bed may not be an ideal time. They may end up going over and over issues once you have left the room and have nothing to distract them - hence why it is so important to consider your child's personality when thinking about when to initiate these talking times.

- **Driving in the car**

Although this option does not give you, as parents, the chance to provide the important eye contact that we discussed, reticent children may feel more able to open up and engage. They may feel less pressure, by being able to look out the window and focus on the world moving past. It can also be helpful as children cannot walk away and refuse to talk to you - although it is important not to push a child to talk, if they are uncomfortable, especially in a situation that they cannot remove themselves from.

- **Walks / walking a dog**

Walking in the fresh air can provide an invaluable opportunity to talk, with the fresh air also supporting clearer thinking processes.

- **Family meetings**

Arranging weekend family meetings can be helpful. Everybody has a chance to vocalise grievances, concerns, worries, or requests.

- **Using resources**

Sometimes the use of sensory resources like clay, putty, slime, or playdough can really encourage a child to open up. It is astounding how many children will appear hesitant to share their thoughts in a Therapy session, until they start playing with a tub of putty - stretching and poking it - seemingly allowing them a feeling of freedom to share more. Just like adults, children can feel self-conscious. The use of a sensory resource, like putty, allows children to manipulate something, without needing to create an end result. It can distract their mind from feelings of discomfort and embarrassment, allowing them to focus on their internal thoughts and expressing these. Colouring, especially the use of adult colouring books, which tend to include in-depth pattern designs, rather than just a plain piece of paper, can also really help with communication.

You may be surprised how much your child shares with you, if you initiate playdough or colouring at home. Make sure you are also engaged, so your child feels like the activity is mutual.

Further points to consider

Just in the same way we discussed your own input and sharing of your own feelings and emotions in the previous chapter, remember that open communication is a two-way street. Why should your child be expected to share with you, if you do not share with them?

Getting into a daily habit of sharing aspects of your own day (even if it feels like your child is not really listening!) is important, as well as now and then sharing your own memories of when you were younger. Being an adult is tough... but so is being a child! Letting your child know that you remember tricky times in your childhood can encourage them to relate to you more.

Your sharing with your child demonstrates your trust in them and this works both ways. A child is more likely to open up when the trust is mutual.

It is also important to remember that it is common for children to feel more comfortable talking to one parent, over another. This is often no reflection on your relationship and although it can be hard not to take it personally, it is in fact a positive that your child is able to share and communicate with one adult within the home, rather than none.

Key 'takeaways' from this chapter to support positive mental health:

- ✓ Consider the importance of listening fully, allowing your child to feel heard, no matter what they are sharing. Why would a child come to you with the 'bigs' if we do not focus on the 'smalls'?
- ✓ Practise developing your own 'active' listening skills
- ✓ Remember not to accidently belittle a child's general worries but consider solution-finding skills instead
- ✓ Consider creating regular 'times to talk' that suit your family's lifestyle and your child's personality
- ✓ Consider your own sharing and communication with your child, developing a two-way trusting relationship

CHAPTER FOUR

Schedules, Clubs and Free-Time

'Unstructured play' (play with no direction, instructions or learning objectives) is not only vital for development, but it also helps a child express what is happening in their inner world and process any issues, concerns, and difficulties, fundamental for positive mental health.

Every child needs to be allowed to have some power and control over what they do. It is a major step in the growing-up process.

Therapeutic Goals to be considered at home:

· Ensuring children have appropriate levels of unstructured free-play within their home environment, as well as suitable periods of time to relax

· Ensuring children have opportunities to demonstrate control, choice and independent decision making

How this builds Positive Mental Health:

· Unstructured, independent play helps a child develop emotional regulation and bodily awareness, whilst encourages the development of creativity and freedom, without always needing pre-determined rules. It supports the development of emotional understanding and self-awareness, whilst expressing inner, personal experiences and feelings

· Unstructured play allows a child to develop new ideas and make mistakes, encouraging a self-belief that they can cope in the future when things go wrong, enabling children to feel resilient and able to bounce back from difficult times

· Opportunities to relax, offers a child's mind and body time to rest and recuperate, ready to face and cope with everyday demands

· Control and choice helps a child understand their own power and abilities, supporting them in becoming aware that they can make positive, healthy, and safe life choices

When I meet a new child for the first time and begin a Therapeutic journey with them, one of the things I like to know is, what does their schedule look like? Do they participate in clubs after school, or on weekends? What does each day of the week feel and look like for them? Not only is this to understand more about who they are as a person and what they enjoy, or dislike, but helps me to create a wider picture of the child's life.

I have had many a conversation with families about activities after school, and whether they are beneficial, or whether it is best for the child to relax after a busy day. I am often asked specifically 'how many' clubs a child should attend, but this is not something I can ever answer, as it is hugely dependent on multiple different factors, unique to each family.

There are many benefits of children attending external clubs and activities away from the home and school environment. Extra-curricular activities offer a child opportunities to try out new things, develop confidence away from their in-school peers, gain new skills and passions and build on their developing identity and self-esteem. Encouraging hobbies from a young age can be so beneficial, as they can mitigate stress, provide opportunities for fun and freedom and offer a distraction from everyday pressures.

Hobbies and clubs after school, or on weekends, therefore, can be viewed as hugely beneficial in helping a child develop positive mental health. However, there are occasions when parents perhaps offer too many opportunities to their children, filling their weekly schedules with plans and not leaving very much 'down time.' I understand for many where this stems from; surely the more our child learns and the more possibilities that are offered to them, the better their future prospects will be?

I have worked with many children whose weekly lives are so busy, moving from one activity to another every day after school / weekends - from swimming, to music lessons, to sports, to tutoring and more. Over time, this persistent pressure of being on the go can actually have an undesirable effect, and greatly lessen the benefits of having hobbies and passions.

This chapter is about taking a step back and re-evaluating your child's schedule. It will explore both ends of the spectrum, examining the potential effects on those with busy schedules, versus the effect on children who appear not to have any passions or hobbies away from school.

It is important to note that mental health is not always negatively affected by having too many, or too little hobbies, but instead I aim to offer you the opportunity to examine the potential effects of both, which you can consider in relation to your child's own personality.

Too many plans?

From my experience, I have observed that intense schedules engaged in regularly over long periods of time, can negatively affect *some* children *later in life,* although, this is not definitive.

During primary school, children may appear to be content and enjoy such a busy lifestyle, but long-term, this can take its toll on the mind, the body and the nervous system, when week on week they do not have sufficient time for unstructured activities and relaxation. I have worked with teenagers whose early childhood was so full of planned and organized extra-curricular activities, that by the time it came to secondary school, they had not developed any skills to learn how to 'switch off' and relax. They were coming to me with very high levels of stress, due to the new pressures of secondary school, and having never learnt internally how to manage 'down time'.

This chapter is not intended to worry you, or to encourage you not to support your child in new hobbies, but its aim is to help you question, ***whether there is sufficient balance in your child's weekly schedule?***

But what is 'balance' and how can we determine whether our child's schedule appears to be too much, too little, or just right?

Exercise one: schedule pie charts

You will need:

- a piece of paper (or use the Notes section)
- some pens
- a spare 15-minutes!

Draw 7 circles, one to represent each day of the week, including weekends. Add segments within each circle, almost as if you were about to draw a clock. Do this according to roughly how many hours your child is up and out of bed for each day; timings may differ on weekends. The following example is a pie chart for a child who is up at around 7.00am and in bed at around 8.00pm.

Image One:

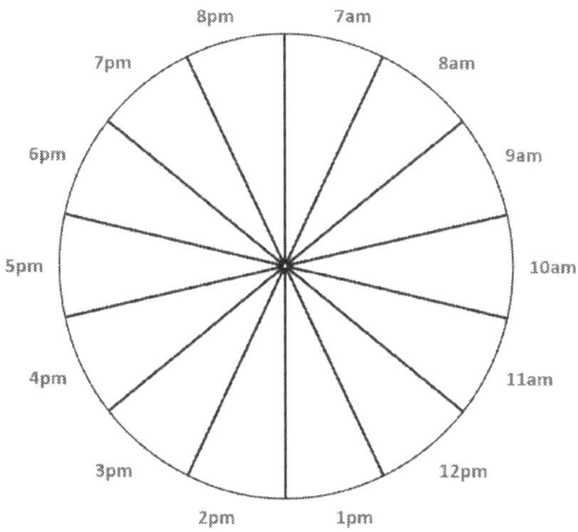

I imagine that for the majority of families, the morning is probably a manic rush getting your child up, ensuring they are dressed, their teeth are brushed, they have had their breakfast, packed their bag and remembered the essentials! For many parents, it may be appropriate to mark the first hour on the circle as 'school-prep'. If, on the other hand, your child is up and ready in 10-minutes, meaning they have an hour to play before school, then add this in as 'free-time'.

Mark in the times your child spends at school and your circle should look something like Image Two. If you come straight home after school, be sure to add in the time you *arrive* at your front door, *not* the time the school day finishes, as some children have a lengthy commute home at the end of each school day. Add some colour to your circle if that helps!

Image Two:

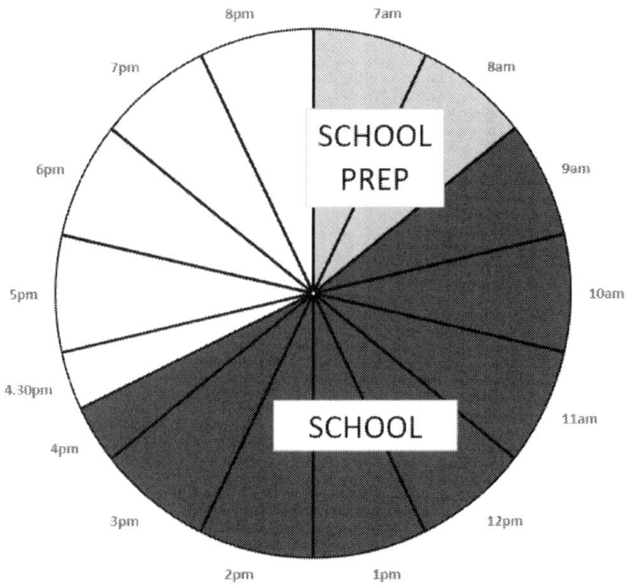

Next, go through each Monday to Friday circle and add in any activities that your child may engage in after school. Remember to include as part of their activity the time taken to travel to and from their clubs and time needed to change into their kit etc.

Then consider, what happens next? Is it dinner? Homework time? Another club? Add all this in, within appropriate time frames, taking care to note exact timings, where possible. Add in any segments of time when your child may have 'free-time'. Does your child have half an hour after their evening meal when they can choose what they want to do, or is it straight into homework and the night-time routine?

Be as honest as you can with your pie charts, otherwise the task will have no benefit.

After dinner / homework or whatever your unique family schedule looks like, end your pie chart at the time your child is *in* bed (regardless of whether they actually fall asleep then, or a little a later on).

Here is an example of what your child's pie charts may be looking like now.

Image Three:

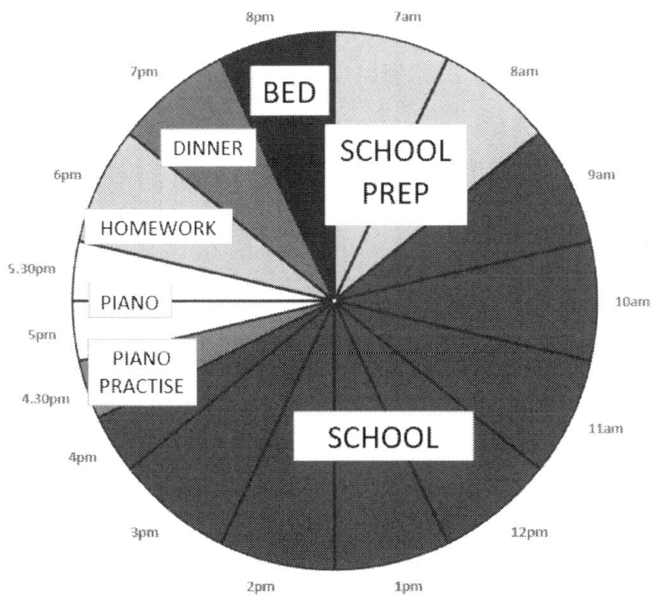

This can also then be carried out for the weekends; although I appreciate things can often change week on week. If you have set plans or commitments each weekend, add these in - if you have time when you always do something out and about together, add this as 'family time'. If your weekends tend to mainly consist of being at home and relaxing, add this as 'free-time'. Now you should have 7 complete pie charts.

Image Four is an example of a child's pie chart who has regular activities on the weekend and Image Five shows an example of a child who does not usually have many weekend plans.

Image Four:

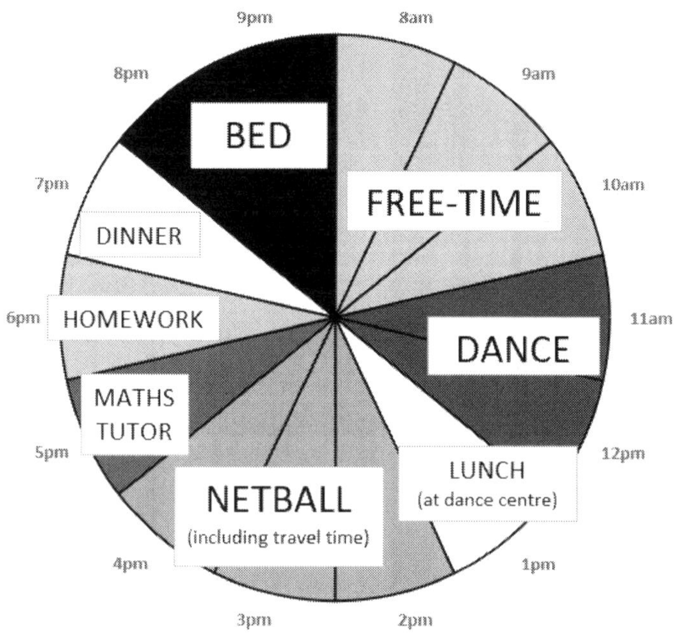

Image Five:

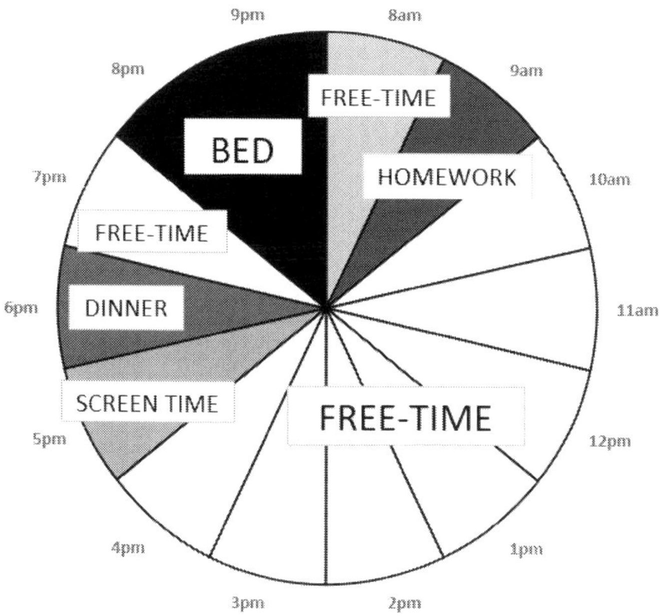

Case Study: Megan aged 8

The following weekly charts belong to Megan; she is 8 and a busy girl! Megan moves from school, to a club, to dinner (often even eating in the car when traffic is heavy on the way home), to quickly having to do her homework, rushing her night-time routine and finally getting into bed around 8.30pm each night. Megan does this every day, Monday to Friday, because she is signed up to daily after school commitments. Megan is usually happy but can get tired and frustrated from time to time, understandably so.

Image Six:

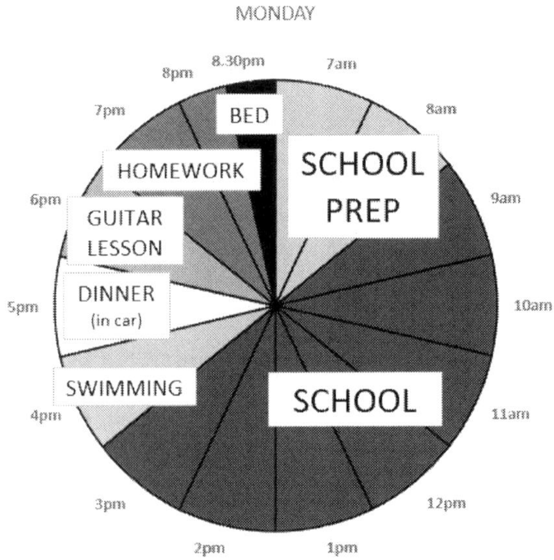
MONDAY
8.30pm
7am
8pm
8am
7pm
BED
HOMEWORK
SCHOOL PREP
9am
6pm
GUITAR LESSON
DINNER (in car)
5pm
10am
SWIMMING
SCHOOL
4pm
11am
3pm
12pm
2pm
1pm

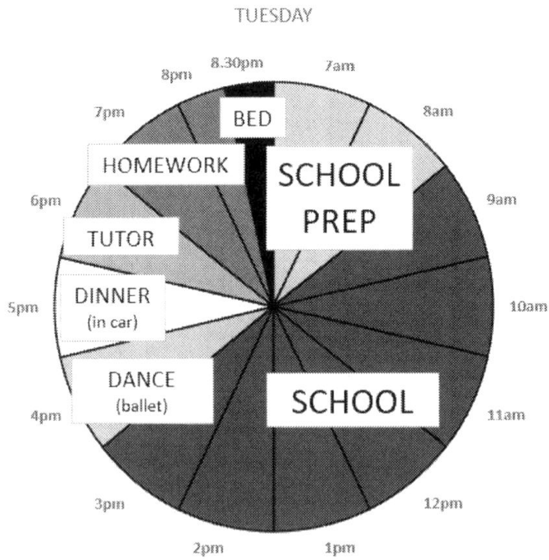
TUESDAY
8.30pm
7am
8pm
8am
7pm
BED
HOMEWORK
SCHOOL PREP
9am
6pm
TUTOR
DINNER (in car)
5pm
10am
DANCE (ballet)
SCHOOL
4pm
11am
3pm
12pm
2pm
1pm

Image Six Continued:

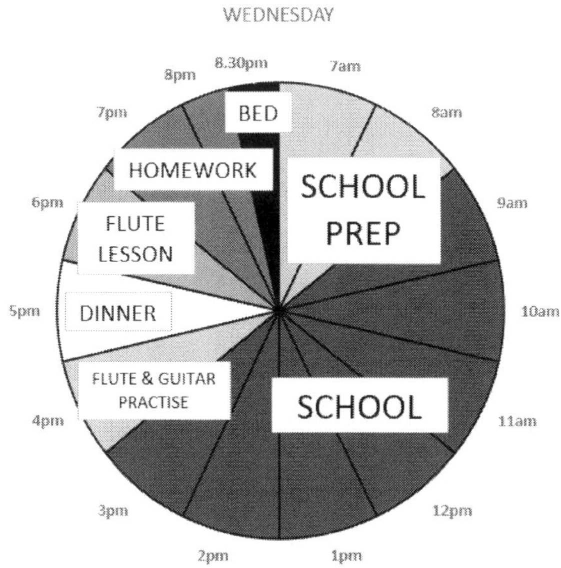

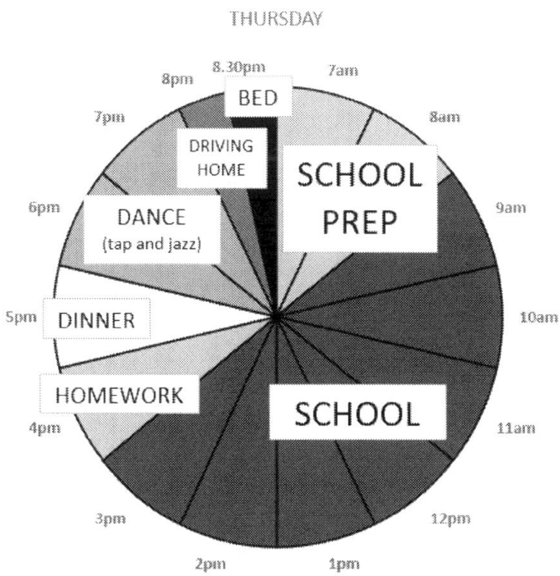

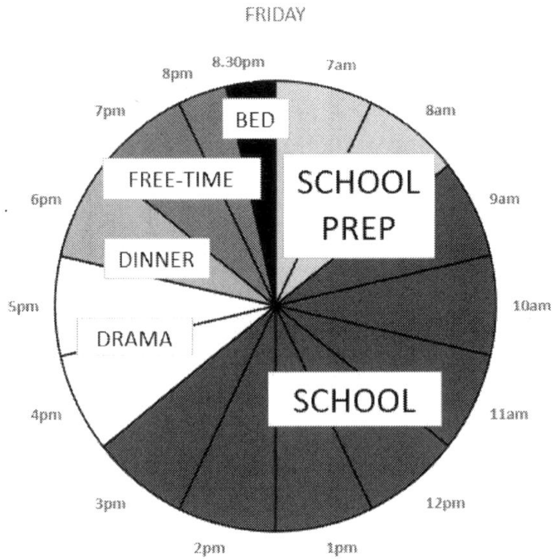

Perhaps from an external perspective we can look at Megan's pie charts and view her as an active, sociable child who has interests, passions, and opportunities provided for her. From a developmental perspective, Megan is keeping fit and active at her dance clubs, is learning fundamental life skills from her swimming, boosting her creativity each week at her two music lessons, is improving her academic attainment via her tutoring and is gaining confidence every Friday by means of her drama group. However, something fundamental is missing from Megan's schedule - she has very limited free-time (only a short amount on a Friday). Her day is mapped out to each exact hour after school, meaning Megan does not have many opportunities to develop her independence and emotional regulation during periods of unstructured time.

Let us fast forward a few years and look at Megan now...

Megan comes to Therapy when she is 14 as her parents are concerned about her anxiety levels, her moods, and that she appears to be frequently stressed.

Megan continues to keep up her extra-curricular activities. During the week she now participates in regular dance classes (she has won countless awards and achieved many dance grades), plays two instruments, of which she has lessons for each week and has a math's tutor every Thursday. Due to her musical talents the school have also encouraged Megan to join their choir and orchestra twice a week, and on top of this Megan is completing her Duke of Edinburgh Award, so volunteers at a local cat shelter once a week. Megan is also about to enter her GCSE year so her workload at school is increasing each term. Sometimes Megan is up until 11.00pm at night just completing her studies. By the time she has showered, packed her bag for school the next day and prepared for bed, it is often close to midnight. Megan has no time to herself and finds it hard to fit in social plans with friends. Her weekends are taken up practising her music and training for dance shows, alongside attempting to catch up on the homework that she was unable to complete during the week.

On the odd weekend, when she may have more free-time and when her parents have encouraged her not to attend clubs, Megan does not know how to relax. She cannot 'switch off' and ends up watching TV all day, feeling d and not wanting to go out, whilst also feeling at she is not being productive or working. School , which you would think would be a welcome break ... udying and the structure of school are a challenge for Megan. She enjoys the first day or two, then cannot bear the lack of structure. Megan does not know what to do with her time, when her weekly plans differ. Megan has never really learnt as a child how to entertain or amuse herself. Boredom was never really something she experienced when she was little; she was always busy. Her days would go by in the blink of an eye, when suddenly it would be bedtime and then the routine would start again the next day. Now if she is bored, Megan finds it unbearable. Megan feels low, moody, and fed up, taking it out on those around her. She feels highly anxious most days due to many stressors, lack of sufficient sleep and attempting to manage her time.

I am in no way suggesting that every child who has a very busy primary school life is going to end up in Therapy like Megan. However, it is worth considering, what the *potential* later effects could be on a child when unstructured free-time and opportunities to be creative via experiencing boredom are not accessible. Potentially, children may miss out on some vital aspects of childhood development, that equip them for their later years and build their resilience and coping strategies for future stressors.

This is where balance comes into play. I am keen to

demonstrate that you can indeed support your child's mental health by striving to create a **balanced life schedule.**

Of course, there are also lots of positives to consider in terms of Megan's lifestyle. She is probably far beyond her years in terms of her skill acquisition. She has an advanced understanding of time management and meeting goals; she can follow structure and has shown huge strength in determination and perseverance. All these are great attributes, especially for future careers - but with lack of balance, in relation to other areas of her life, it is important to consider how important all these attributes really are, long-term, in relation to physical and mental health?

So, what is balance?

Let us go back to your pie charts again. Highlight in bold the times that you wrote 'free-time' on each of your child's daily schedules. How many hours does this add up to?

In an ideal situation, our general rule of thumb should be that a child should have opportunities *every single day* for 'free-time', to make their own choices and to have control over what they select to do. Naturally, if your child has one busy day in a week with lots of other opportunities for free-time, then this is OK, but just be considerate over the whole school week, how much of a child's schedule allows for this.

It does not matter, so much, how your child uses this free-time, so long as they have the chance to do something *independently* of their own choice. They may decide to play in their room, watch television, play on the computer (within the boundaries regarding technology you have set with them), draw / colour, play with their neighbour, or run around in the garden. They may choose to watch TV because they are tired, or they may decide to colour or draw because they find it relaxing. They may wish to play with their toys because it has been a stressful day and want to enact it out with a battle between Mr Dinosaur and Mr Cow. On the other hand, they may want to play outside because it has felt like they have been cooped in all day at school. Whatever they do with this time, they are learning to select an activity because they 'need' to do it and are developing this imperative understanding to respond to their *body's needs.* Even if your child is moaning at you during their free-time that they are 'bored', this time is still essentially so important, as it is allowing them opportunities to use their own ideas, adapt, be creative and rely solely on themselves - imperative for creating one of our fundamental Therapy goals of self-belief. Boredom also allows the part of our brain to develop which allows for integrative thinking (deeper, more thoughtful thinking, in terms of solutions and ideas).

It is important to note that screen time would not be considered as 'unstructured play', but likely to be something many children would choose to select if they had the choice. If all your child chooses to engage with during their free-time is screens / technology, then you may like to consider placing limits on this, to ensure they still have suitable access to unstructured play. This will all be discussed in our 'Technological Usage' chapter.

Questions for parents to consider:

When examining your pie charts, perhaps take a moment to think about and discuss together if you have a partner, the following questions. If your child's schedule is fairly empty, the questions may not apply, however we will be exploring sparse pie charts very soon within this chapter.

Does my child need to do all these activities?

What is the goal for them participating in these clubs? Is it for me, or for them?

Do they rush to them excitedly each week, or are they tired and asking not to go?

Did my child request to join the club, or did I tell them to?

Should any clubs be moved or changed?

If my child loves doing this activity, but it makes the whole day stressful and rushed, can we move it to the weekend, so they have lots of time on either side for free-time?

Is there a way of amending our evening routine slightly so my child can have 30-minutes to relax after dinner?

If your child has mostly free weekends, but a busy weekday schedule, then this is still allowing for free-time each week, but it could be an idea to try and allow a little more of this unstructured time into the weekday routine too. School can be stressful for some children, so only having this free-time on weekends, is sometimes not quite enough.

Maybe your day-to-day plans vary substantially each week. If so, be consciously aware, each week, of when your child is accessing this essential unstructured time. Should you notice your child has had a particularly busy week, and as a one-off they have had limited free-time or unstructured play, perhaps change, or cancel your weekend plans. Initiate a pyjama day, do not leave the house all day and let your children play to their hearts content. If you feel you have little control in the week, due to school schedules, homework, or school commitments, try to at least have control over your weekend. Although long-term this is probably not enough, one full day of relaxation with free-play and no plans can help re-set a child's body over the weekend, ready to start afresh again on Monday.

It is important to remember that there is no exact right or wrong here - it is about being aware and consciously considering each week, your children's plans, and monitoring them as your child develops.

Genre of activities

Another idea to consider is the *type* of activities your child engages in. Are they all competitive, leading up to achievements, or exams, or are they just for fun?

For example, a dance class whereby a child is working towards dance exams, is very different to a dance class which your child is attending for pure enjoyment and to keep physically fit. It is important, where possible, to create not just a balance in relation to *time* each week, but a balance of competitiveness / goal orientated activities and those which focus on enjoyment and being in the moment.

Of course, for some children working towards a grade or exam can also be beneficial in terms of having a motivation, aim and becoming self-driven. Having extra-curricular activities which are simply for fun and have no competitive nature whatsoever, for example yoga classes or fitness groups, are also positive.

Having all activities which are achievement-based and focused around examinations, grades and winning, can set up a child to internalise feelings of self-worth, that are based on their achievements, and not their personality or behaviour. The number of families who contact me whose child appears to put so much pressure on themselves and only feel good when they are top of the class, or get an A+ in exams is alarming. It is important for mental health for children to have pride in themselves, and their personality, separate from their accomplishments. We will explore this further in our 'Making Mistakes, Failures and Coping When Things Go Wrong' chapter.

In summary:

1. Create honest diagrams of your child's weekly schedules

2. Assess the timings of your child's schedule and if there are suitable amounts of free-time

3. Assess the goal-orientated nature of your child's schedule

If need be, you may want to consider changing your child's weekly schedule slightly. This may feel like a daunting task, but actually in the grand scheme of overall mental health, small changes like this now, during the primary school years, can make a fundamental difference to a child's well-being in the future.

The other end of the spectrum

Perhaps if all your child's pie charts only contain 'school' and 'free-time', it could be worth discussing with them if there may be any extra-curricular activities that they would like to try. Supporting children in having a go at new things and engaging in hobbies can be especially beneficial for mental health (if scheduled within a balance).

From a physical health perspective, (physical health fundamentally links to overall mental health), it is worth also considering if your child is getting enough *physical* activity in their schedule. According to the NHS, at the time of publishing, a child should have on average 60-minutes a day of 'moderate physical activity' each week. This can include things like, walking to school, playground games, riding a scooter, walking the dog or skateboarding.

For some children, trying something new, can be daunting at first, although it may in the long run be a positive change. If your child is hesitant to engage in activities outside of school, here are a few pointers to consider:

1. Encourage your child to join a club in school, either at lunchtime, or after school. They will be in an environment that is familiar to them and perhaps down the line they may feel more confident to then try an out of school activity.

2. If you are encouraging your child to try something outside of school, perhaps see if there is a friend or classmate who already attends a club; sometimes having one familiar face can really help a child feel more relaxed and at ease.

3. Agree with your child that they will try out the club a certain number of times and if they do not like it, they do not have to go back. If possible, try to get them to agree to attend at least two or three times. Attending something just once, often does not give a true impression of what the club entails, especially if your child feels very nervous at the start - two or

three times helps give a clearer perspective.

4. Consider the size of the group; if your child is overly anxious about trying something new, try to find an activity that has a small number of children attending. Build this up, over time, to a larger group activity.

5. Chat openly to your child about what would make them feel better about attending, for example, would they like you to wait on site?

6. If your child does attend something that made them initially feel nervous, offer lots of positive praise afterwards.

7. If possible, before attending something they are worried about, remind your child of other occasions when they felt nervous and how well they coped. Showing that *you* are confident in their abilities, can help increase their internal confidence. Try not to show your child your own anxiety.

8. Do not worry too much if your child is *still* not keen on participating in extra-curricular activities - give it

a break and try again in a term or so. Forcing them to continue may make them anxious and stressed. In this case you could support interests at home - from cooking, sewing, coding, online dance routines to animal care and more. To support your child's self-belief, self-esteem and help them gain new skills, you, as parents can play an important role within the home environment!

Offering control and choice

It is important for all children to learn that they have 'control' and 'choice' over some of their decisions. This supports them in developing their own self-awareness and internal self-belief, as well as encouraging positive vital life choices as they grow – all fundamental aspects of positive mental health.

Choice and control help children feel empowered, an important feeling for a primary aged child. A child who has never experienced any feeling of empowerment, is likely to struggle, as they get older, if they do not possess the confidence to know they can independently make positive and powerful decisions. At the same time, in order to feel secure and contained, children also need to know that the adults around them will provide the basic structure and will make the 'key' family decisions. It is vital not to put pressure on a child to make any form of decision around an important family matter, or dynamic, especially in regards to serious family conflicts or marital difficulties. Instead, consider what sort of opportunities for *appropriate decision making* you can offer. As with children's schedules, control and choice needs to be within a balance. For younger children, in early primary school, you may like to offer them two choices to support independent thinking. Older children may feel more adept at making certain choices independently, without having narrowed down options.

There are some children who are happy to go with the flow and comply with whatever their parent decides. Others wish to be more involved, are more assertive and push to have their voice heard. Whatever the nature of your child, empower them with a certain amount of choice and control beyond their unstructured free-play.

Some examples could be:

Would you like jam or cheese in your sandwich?

Shall we go to the park before the library, or after?

Would you like a 10-minute break before homework, or would you like to get it done now?

Which book out of these two shall we read tonight?

Shall we use crayons or pens to write the birthday card?

Do not forget it is important at times, to ask your child for help.

It is human instinct to want to be needed, and this is just

the same for children as it is for adults. Seeing an adult ask them for help, can be highly empowering for a child, understanding that mum / dad respect and value their assistance. This can go a long way in helping a child to develop an internal belief and can also help them feel confident in their own decision making as they grow.

Even if you do not really need their help, try and get into a pattern once a week of asking your child for some assistance or advice!

Key 'takeaways' from this chapter to support positive mental health:

✓ Assess your child's daily schedule, ensuring there are opportunities for unstructured play, down time and relaxation

✓ Consider your child's hobbies, or lack of hobbies, and whether these are goal-orientated or just for fun

✓ Consider the importance of providing your child with opportunities for independent decision making, control and choice

CHAPTER FIVE

Developing Positive Sleep Patterns

Therapeutic Goals to be considered at home:

· Ensuring children experience a regular and consistent routine, developing a sense of security in terms of knowing what to expect

· Ensuring children develop positive sleep patterns and regularly achieve the recommended number of hours sleep per night, according to guidance

How this builds Positive Mental Health:

· Security and an understanding of expectation can reduce a child's stress and anxiety levels and build a feeling of safety, trust, and resilience

· Positive sleep patterns can result in a child experiencing improved moods and enhanced thought processes to cope with stressors. Self-esteem and self-belief can be increased, in terms of identity awareness, abilities and academia, through better concentration, memory and focus. Sleep fundamentally supports so much in relation to positive mental health!

A key aspect of Therapy with children is ensuring the process for them is consistent, allowing a routine to develop. Children attend their sessions always on the same day and time each week, with the same Therapist, in the same room, with the same equipment. Certain boundaries within the Therapeutic relationship are consistently followed, allowing children to develop a certain understanding around expectations. Quite simply, consistency develops a feeling of security; a child who feels secure and knows what to expect is able to better manage and cope during times of stress, greatly benefiting overall mental health - these Therapeutic goals are something that parents, with a little support, can easily achieve at home.

Routine, expectations, and consistent parenting are important to strive for, throughout all aspects of childhood. Consistency and routine are arguably most important when it comes to sleep and establishing positive sleep routines. The primary school years are when we can solidify appropriate understanding of sleep regimes, which will greatly benefit children as they grow and develop.

Something which I have frequently noted, is many children that I work with have some form of struggle when it comes to sleep. Whether that be difficulty falling asleep or difficulty in maintaining sleep throughout the night.

In today's society, poor, or disturbed sleep is something which is very common, and I am sure there are multiple children in every classroom who come into school each day, having not reached the recommended number of hours sleep for their age. Technology, screen time, school pressures, homework, busy schedules, playdates, parent-working hours and general anxieties, are some reasons why sleep can become hugely impacted.

Busy lives and general family dynamics mean that often, night-time routines and timings can sometimes be hard to adhere to. Although a flexible evening routine here and there is OK - long-term, this can cause difficulties.

Interestingly, when a child comes to Therapy unable to sleep, I have to determine whether poor mental health is influencing their sleep, or whether a lack of, or disturbed sleep is causing poor mental health. Sleep and mental health are so finely linked.

I am sure we can all associate low moods and feelings of irritability with having a poor night's sleep, or recall times of difficulty, particularly when your child was a baby, when your sleep was disrupted over a longer period of time. However, long-term sleep deprivation can stretch far beyond just affecting our mood. The continued lack of it can have vast detrimental effects on our immune system, appetite, weight, emotion management, thought processes, academic performance, memory, focus, reactions, and general overall well-being, thus greatly impacting mental health. In short, adults and children who are consistently over-tired cannot function properly.

Ongoing difficulties with disturbed sleep undoubtedly leads to a cycle that is often difficult to break, without support.

The following figures show the recommended minimum and maximum number of hours of sleep that children of different ages need (per a 24-hour period) on a *regular* basis, to ensure *optimum health.*

These figures were published by Great Ormond Street, in 2017, compiled by the American Academy of Sleep Medicine (AASM) and were reviewed again in 2020.

· Children 3 to 5 years: 10 - 13 hours of sleep (including naps)

· Children 6 to 12 years: 9 - 12 hours of sleep

· Teenagers 13 to 18 years: 8 - 10 hours of sleep

It is important to initially consider the *minimum* number of hours sleep for your child's age, and ask yourself - is my child getting an adequate amount each night? This must *not* include their reading time, but from the time they actually fall asleep.

Similarly, if your child is asleep at around 9.00pm each night and wakes at around 7.00am, but is often awake for two hours in the middle of the night due to sleep disturbances, this awake time must be taken off the overall time calculated.

Do also consider, that due to the differences in the figures for each age range, the minimum number of hours sleep, listed previously, is not always enough for some children. Different children, with different personalities and schedules, may need above the minimum number of hours in order to function appropriately the next day. If your child is experiencing any of the difficulties mentioned in this chapter, then that may be a sign, (even if they are reaching the *minimum* number of hours sleep for their age), that this may not be quite enough. It is also crucial to remember that these number of hours each night, must be achieved regularly - so a child who may sleep well two or three times a week, but poorly four or five times a week, is not achieving their desired number of sleep hours, *consistently*.

It could be worth assessing your child's sleep schedule over the next week or two, to work out how many hours on average they are getting each night, in order to give you a fuller picture. Sometimes just looking back on the past week will give inaccurate results, whereas actually taking the time to examine this each night, over a longer period of time, can give you clearer answers about your child's sleep patterns and thus determine if you need to make any adjustments. You could jot this down in the 'Notes' section at the back of this book, as a 'sleep diary', to determine whether any of the ideas in this chapter would be useful to implement.

One thing that is difficult to ascertain is the 'quality' of sleep a child gets. A child who may be worried, or has developed a pattern of waking up and lying in bed over-thinking, may 'technically' be in bed and seem to be sleeping well, but actually may in fact not be getting sufficient, good quality sleep for their age. The chapters 'Encouraging Open Communication' and 'Expressing Feelings and Emotions' offer ideas to help with worry.

Sleep, behavioural patterns, and self-esteem

Generally, when I have children coming to see me with behavioural concerns, I often find that they are getting far below the recommended guidelines of sleep each night, for their age. Furthermore, many parents are often convinced their child may have a diagnosable condition, such as ADHD (Attention Deficit Hyperactivity Disorder) which is causing challenging behaviour. After Therapeutic work and making positive sleep changes at home, often that behaviour is reversed, and no diagnosis is necessary (although of course this is not always the case). Interestingly though, some of the signs linking to ADHD can also be very similar to the signs of a highly over-tired child. Children who are consistently over-tired, experience a release in the hormone 'adrenaline', which can make them seem to be hyperactive. It can be confusing, as surely an over-tired child, should *appear* tired and want to rest? However, in fact, from an observational viewpoint, that child appears to have huge surges in energy, often bouncing around before bed!

I have additionally noted that children having difficulties with their peers, or low self-esteem have often also been having inadequate levels of sleep, over a prolonged period of time.

The following case study demonstrates how easy it is for mental health decline to escalate, affecting multiple areas of a child's life, simply due to lack of sleep.

Case Study: Ben aged 7

For a long time, Ben has struggled with sleep. His parents feel they have tried everything, but without fail every single night after being put to bed, Ben refuses to sleep. He will call out, try to engage in conversation through a multitude of questions and when that does not work, he will frequently come downstairs to 'check' on mum / dad. Ben does not fall asleep until at least 10.30pm each night, sometimes even later. When mum / dad try to wake Ben in the morning, he struggles to get up; he is exhausted, and it becomes an effort just to get Ben out of bed. He is moody at breakfast time and will not listen to instructions, causing sibling arguments and frustration escalates as the morning routine goes on. Getting out of the house is a manic rush, with shouting from all and a panicked scurry to ensure everyone is out the door on time.

At a recent parents' evening, Ben's teacher comments on his behaviour at school, sharing with mum / dad that he has difficulties listening in class and does at times disrupt his peers. Ben is doing fairly well at school, but is struggling with maths and English and is falling behind slightly.

A week later mum / dad receive a call from school saying Ben has been in a fight and has pushed one of his peers off the slide in the playground. They are asked to go into school for a meeting to see how all can work together to address Ben's escalating inappropriate behaviour. The teacher shares further concerns on how Ben struggles to focus in class. She describes him as fidgety and at times hyperactive. Talk turns to whether Ben may have any additional concerns that need addressing, such as ADHD.

Mum / dad leave the meeting drained and upset - they did not realise things had got so bad. Ben may not listen sometimes at home, but he is a good boy and they are surprised by what was said. The school advises mum / dad to see a GP regarding some possible psychological support or assessment. The GP advises them that the waiting list is very long and suggests that they may like to seek help from a mental health professional who specialises in children.

Ben is a happy, engaging little boy when I meet him and is so excited to explore the Therapy room. I am aware that Ben's parents have expressed concerns about possible ADHD, however my role is not to officially diagnose, but to offer children an outlet for their thoughts and emotions. Although Ben seems to express a desire to exert energy, my initial sense is that Ben does not fit the further patterns of a child with ADHD - although of course a diagnosis can be complex. After working together and playing together, it appears part of the concern, is Ben's struggle with how he views himself, combined with low self-esteem.

Now let us take a moment to look at the same scenario, but from the possible perspective of Ben.

Ben has not slept well for many, many weeks, maybe even months and he knows how badly mum / dad want him to sleep and be a good boy. Ben feels anxious when his evening meal finishes as he knows that it is almost bedtime - Ben can sense mum is worried that he will not sleep, and he does not want to make her fed up again. Mum quickly remembers it is spellings tomorrow, so they spend the next 10-minutes going through the words that Ben needs to remember. He gets 4 wrong out of 10 and feels silly, although mum does say he is doing well, Ben does not feel he is. His little sister keeps screaming for her bottle and dad is quickly trying to help her, whilst also needing to do a call for work that evening. Things are all a little rushed. Bath time is fun - there is splashing, but maybe too much splashing, the floor gets a little wet and mum gets slightly annoyed. Pyjamas on, Ben is feeling anxious, he hates the bit when the lights go out and he knows that it is coming soon. It is dad's turn tonight for the story - it is a funny one! After the story dad tucks Ben in, kisses and hugs him and reminds him to be a good boy and go to sleep. Mum comes in gives Ben a kiss and reminds him to stay in his bed and then he will get a treat tomorrow. They leave the room. It is dark and Ben feels lonely. He is wide awake and knows he will not sleep for ages. He waits a few minutes then suddenly remembers he needs to ask mum something about their plans for tomorrow - he also wants to tell dad something funny that his friend did today. Ben feels thirsty, now he needs the loo! He is up about five times; mum is telling him to go to sleep, dad is too - by the time it is trip number seven, mum and dad are getting angry. He goes back to his bed, feeling upset and the next thing he knows he can hear the birds chirping outside his window, the light is creeping in through the blind and mum is giving him a kiss on his head telling him it is time to get up. Through blinkered eyes he sees mum's smiling face, then within seconds he is back to sleep again, before the regular morning routine of mum / dad coaxing him out of bed begins. The whispered, loving words to get Ben up, changes into mum's frantic, panicked voice and the next thing he is up, eating breakfast with one eye closed, and dad telling him to hurry as they have to be out the house in 20-minutes. There is no time to finish his cereal, then it is teeth, uniform on, shoes on, out the door, quick quick quick...

Ben is excited to get to school - he loves his friends, especially Luka whom he has known since nursery. They have a 10-minute playground break before registration, so play catch and hide and seek with some boys in the year above, then head into class. It is art first, Ben likes art - then it is science, followed by maths. Ben hates maths and it is still an hour until lunchtime. He is hungry and tired. His head hurts a little and his eyes feel heavy. Now the teacher is bombarding him with questions about subtraction and addition and he cannot work out exactly what they mean. Sara, next to him, is on question ten, he is on question three. Ben cannot focus and is fed up - the numbers are silly, and he hates them. The teacher then goes through the sheet and tells them to mark their friend's answers. Sara has 10 out of 10. Sara then uses her extra sharp red pencil and marks crosses on Ben's work before handing it back to him. Ben got 3 out of 10 correct. The teacher comes and collects them and raises her eyebrows at Ben, saying he should have done better. Ben feels silly, and angry and annoyed that Sara did so well, and he did not. Why does this keep happening - why does his brain not let him get all the answers right? Ben feels mad at his own brain. He feels rubbish.

It is lunchtime - finally time for some food - Ben is starving. Lunch is good and then it is playtime. The boys play catch again and it is Ben's turn to be the chaser - he runs after the boys laughing, then Fred sticks his tongue out and says, "you can't catch me, you are rubbish at catching!" Ben says he is not playing anymore and the game teeters off as the other boys get distracted in activities around the playground. Ben and Luka move to the climbing frame and see Fred climbing up the steps to the mini slide. "Catch me now Ben! Bet you can't!" Ben is angry again and sees red. Ben does not quite know what happens, but the next minute Fred is on the floor crying and Ben is sitting opposite Mr Franklin, the headmaster. He is telling Ben his behaviour is not acceptable and asking him why he would do that.

Fast forward 2-hours and he is in the car with mum / dad who are telling him they are disappointed in his behaviour and asking him why he would want to hurt someone. They look sad and Ben feels sad. Ben is confused; he also does not know why. He did not want to hurt Fred, but he did not feel quite right inside, but cannot explain it. Maybe there is something wrong with him...?

The previous two examples show how simple it is for behaviour to escalate when a child is over-tired, and when examining Ben's perspective, how easy it is for patterns of behaviour to link into one another, causing a spiralling effect.

Often when a child comes to me because of their behaviour, one of the most important aspects of our sessions is working through the way they may internally view themselves and their own levels of self-esteem. Young children are developing their sense of self every day, through interactions and experiences. This sense of self is fragile and malleable, meaning if a child is constantly getting into trouble (for Ben this was simply because he could not control his behaviour when he was exhausted) their sense of self is developing around a feeling of constantly doing things which are seen as 'bad'.

Ben's teachers and parents have not done anything wrong and Ben needs to learn what is acceptable and what is not, especially in terms of the safety of other children. What is happening here is a very common chain of events, with one behaviour leading into another, causing a downward spiral. This constant negativity around bedtime, school and his behaviour, is resulting in Ben's sense of self becoming affected - all very much likely due to long-term lack of sleep. Ben's mood, appetite, focus, academia, behaviour, friendships, self-belief, and overall mental health are all impacted - simply because he needs more sleep.

The reaction of Ben's peers is common for this age group and a well-slept, more resilient child would be able to cope with a comment of this kind from Fred. However, for a child who is sleep deprived, when comments are tapping in and reflecting their own inner critic (for Ben, this was that he is 'rubbish') then of course most children are likely to respond inappropriately. I am not stating that for every child who lacks sleep, this pattern will occur, but this common example shows how easily models of behaviour can develop through sleep deprivation, which can influence so many factors of childhood mental health.

As well as supporting his decreasing self-esteem, Ben's parents needed some support in adjusting his night-time routine, providing a calmer setting before bedtime, and helping to reduce his anxiety. We will discuss all of this and how you can create an ideal 'sleep environment' later on in the chapter.

If you have any concerns about your child's learning abilities, self-belief, self-esteem, behaviours and friendships, it is *always* worth initially examining their sleep patterns.

If you have no concerns about your child's sleep, it is still worth reading on, as developing and fine-tuning positive habits throughout primary school can go a long way in teaching children these fundamental skills for later on in life - imperative for the secondary school years. With anything child-related, it is always worth assessing, even if you have no concerns, whether an odd change, or slightly amending something, may add *extra* benefit overall.

Taking care of *yourself*

We do have to briefly consider your own sleep patterns and your own behaviours around sleep first, before we can contemplate amending or examining your child's sleep patterns.

It can be common for parents who suffer from fatigue and tiredness to also have a child who may struggle with factors relating to sleep. Quite simply, it may feel impossible for a parent to find a remedy to break the pattern of their child's sleeping problems, if they are so tired themselves. Trying to find a solution can be exhausting.

Pressures on parents today are extreme, especially throughout the primary school years when your child is still highly dependent on you for almost everything they do. It is no wonder so many parents are sleep deprived when they are juggling a child's peer relationships, their homework and hobbies, family dynamics, work, and their own social commitments. This begs the question, how can a parent support their child's overall mental health, if theirs may be in decline, due to lack of, or poor sleep?

Points to consider:

How much sleep are *you* actually getting each night?

Of course, sleep requirements vary greatly from person to person, but most healthy adults generally need between 7-9-hours of sleep per night, in order to function at their best. On an average week, are you getting this most nights? Remember, just as we discussed in relation to children, two or three good nights of sleep, and four or five poor nights, does not equate to an overall balance.

There are certain aspects that are also important for *you* to consider as an adult too, in terms of your schedule, diet and general evening routine.

Take into consideration if you have time to relax each evening before you go to bed. Do you have time every night, even if it is just for half an hour to relax, read and unwind?

Are you often on your phone or device close to the time you turn out your light? Facts around 'melatonin' and screen time that we will shortly explore, in relation to children, also apply to adults too!

Are you able to offer yourself opportunities, even if it is just once or twice a week, to spend more time doing something you particularly enjoy, either in or out of the home? Often engaging with passions and hobbies can act as a fundamental distraction away from stressors, helping us to sleep better, for example sewing, reading, yoga or swimming. Stressors and over-thinking, for both adults and children can affect sleep, and participating in things that we enjoy can be a welcome interruption for our minds. As parents, it is likely we spend a considerable amount of time helping our children to find and master their own passions, but it is important as adults to have time for your own interests too - as an adult, and a parent, you are allowed interests that do not involve your child!

If you have a partner, is it possible for you to take turns with your child's evening / sleep routine, so that you can have some time for yourselves every other night?

Please do take a few moments to bear in mind all the previous points, as we will now go back to focusing on your child.

Sleep hygiene

When we discuss sleep, what is important to examine is your child's 'Sleep Hygiene' - contrary to how it sounds, this is nothing to do with cleanliness, or clean sheets, but is in fact the *lead up and routine* around your child's bedtime.

Positive sleep hygiene can make a fundamental difference to how well a child settles and manages to stay asleep throughout the night - which in turn hugely affects their physical and emotional health. There are many aspects that make up sleep hygiene, which will all be discussed, including routine, diet, screen time, wind-down time, temperature, lighting, noise levels and self-settling skills. It may sound confusing and daunting, considering all these points, but hopefully the following paragraphs will demonstrate simple ways to improve your child's sleep hygiene.

The sleep environment

When it comes to ensuring your child is getting the sleep they need, their 'sleep environment' plays a key factor. If you think about your own sleep environment, there are probably certain conditions which make it more conducive for you to get to sleep. Your child is the same. For example, for some, it can be difficult to relax in an untidy, cluttered room. To encourage your child to remain in bed, consider, is there anything particular your child likes near them? Is there a teddy they want to cuddle? Do they have a drink at hand? By creating the 'perfect' sleep environment, you are setting the stage for success. The following pointers also discuss further aspects to create an optimal sleep environment.

Lighting

Managing your child's exposure to light in their bedroom is essential in creating a healthy sleep environment. When your child goes to sleep, it is important to have their room as dark as possible. Darkness helps to release melatonin, the body's 'sleep hormone'. Not only does this hormone help us to go to sleep initially, but it also helps us stay asleep for longer overnight. Where possible, you want to try to prevent natural light sneaking in around the edges of the curtains. Even brief exposure to light can interfere with sleep. Blackout blinds are perfect for blocking out any unwanted light and creating a dark sleep environment. If these are too expensive or unsuitable for your child's room, try spraying the windows with water and pressing pre-cut tin foil to the windows - although this is only a temporary solution. You could see if this makes a difference, over a consistent 2-week period, before then looking into purchasing something more long-term.

During the evening routine, try to switch the main lights off straight after bath time, as your child is putting their pyjamas on and getting into bed. Replace this with just a small side light or a light outside the room, so that you can still see what you are doing. Bright lights during the pre-bedtime routine can stimulate the brain and stop our bodies from entering a relaxed, pre-sleep state. Small changes like this will assist in the development of your child's sleep cycles.

Some children like to sleep with a dim light on and this is quite common. Very young children often cannot understand the difference between reality and fantasy and therefore genuinely believe (no matter how much we reason with them), that there could be a monster under the bed, or imagine a shadow to be something scary and sinister. If your child cannot sleep without some light, I would suggest using a night light away from your child's bed. Purchase the dimmest possible light source; red light bulbs are the least disruptive to your child's circadian rhythm (day and night cycles) as white and blue lights suppress the production of melatonin - the hormone that makes us feel sleepy.

Temperature

Your child's sleep environment should be a comfortable temperature between 18 to 22 degrees Celsius. It can sometimes be difficult to judge this, therefore using a room thermometer can be useful. Children (and adults) can be greatly affected by weather changes, and for some, it can be highly disruptive sleeping in a room that feels too hot, or too cold.

Noise

Your child's sleep environment should be quiet, therefore you should limit the noise in the house as bedtime is approaching, helping your child's mind and body prepare for sleep. If you find it difficult to keep the noise levels down, especially if there are other siblings in the house, you can help block sounds out by using a calming playlist, or a white noise machine. A white noise machine can produce several consistent soft sounds such as ocean waves, which are known to help calm and de-stress children. There are also apps that you can download, that tell 'sleep stories' to children. Often these are more beneficial than just listening to an audio telling of a story they enjoy, as the latter can sometimes excite and keep children awake, being eager to find out what happened next.

Distractions

Keeping your child's room free from distractions lets them focus on their sleeping. When putting your child down after a calm, quiet routine the last thing you want to do is offer activities that capture their attention and increase their alertness such as iPads, video games and television. It is important to separate sleep time from activities that can cause excitement. It may also be worth considering the books that your child reads before bedtime - I have worked with many children who love a murder mystery, or detective series, yet this can actually sometimes keep a child awake, stimulating their brain further. If your child has no qualms falling asleep, then of course stick to the books that they enjoy, but the genre of book may be important to consider for some.

Children can also be highly stimulated by the toys in their room which can distract them from sleeping - you may need to consider removing some of these close to bedtime, or if you are fortunate to have another room in your house as a playroom, perhaps consider keeping the exciting toys in there.

Routine

You may or may not already have in place a clear and consistent evening routine, but establishing a bedtime schedule for your child can be the key to creating good sleep habits. A calming routine which follows a predictable pattern helps signal 'it is time to go to sleep'. It will also allow your child to feel safe and reassured as they will always know what is about to happen next. It is important your bedtime routine is not too short or too long; 30 / 45-minutes should be enough time for them to wind-down from the day, but not enough to allow your child to become over-tired. Over-tired children experience a release of adrenaline which interferes with the body's production of melatonin, the sleep-inducing hormone, meaning that an over-tired child, can in fact, often not fall asleep.

A simple routine each night can involve wind-down time, a calming bath / shower, some reading time and a cuddle and a kiss. If you have more than one floor in your house, it can be an idea once your child has gone upstairs to begin the evening routine, to try and limit them returning downstairs again, so they get into the pattern of knowing bedtime is approaching.

Interestingly, what happens in the run up to bedtime, hugely impacts how a child falls asleep and whether they are likely to stay asleep throughout the night. Even if your child currently does sleep well, it is still always worth considering the pre-bedtime routine and if certain adjustments may be beneficial. Remember, routine and consistency help a child feel secure. A child who feels a positive sense of security is far more able to cope with stressors and challenges in life.

During this 30 / 45-minute bedtime routine, make sure that you avoid:

Screen time, homework, school related matters, (for example getting PE kits ready and packing school bags for the next day), sibling conflict, eating of snacks, exercise (unless it is some form of gentle stretches / yoga).

This period each evening is a time for your child's mind and body to relax, switch off, feel calm and prepare for sleep.

An idea which can be useful for any primary aged child (if you cater for it in an age-appropriate way) is to have a 'bedtime box' or 'quiet time box' that is brought out each day, at this time.

This is a small box with resources that you have organised for your child and there are special 'rules' which apply. It is important that you explain to your child that it is a 'special box' of activities just for this time. Keep the box up on a shelf where they cannot access it during the daytime.

- To make sure your child does not get bored, try to rotate the activities in the box on a regular basis, every few weeks or so.

- Find a special area where this time takes place; you could consider putting the box on a certain rug / mat which represents 'quiet time'.

- Make sure the lights are dimmed during this time to help your child ease into quietly playing.

- Try to be as creative as possible to make these activities different to their daytime games.

- Ideas for this box:

Simple building structures like LEGO®, colour by number books, sticker books, playdough, sensory putty, jigsaw puzzles, threading or sewing activities, knitting, stretch and squeeze toys, dot-to-dot pictures, magazines that suit their interests, simple model kits, maze puzzles, drawing activities or colouring books. For older children adult colouring books are wonderful, as they include a range of patterns, which can help calm the mind.

More mature primary school children may not need a physical box, but instead just a list of choices that they can engage with at this time. The general rule of thumb is that ideally, children should play alone (unless they rarely fight with their sibling) and activities should be relaxing, calming and not over excite children. With busy after school schedules and homework, this time does not have to be long - getting into a habit of offering your child this wind-down time for 15 / 20-minutes before bath time is enough.

After this wind-down period, it is time to start the bedtime routine, which ideally should consist of a bath or shower, teeth, bed, story time or independent reading, a cuddle, a kiss and lights out. Make sure your child goes to the toilet as the last thing they do before bed, to prevent night-time waking.

Of course, things can be relaxed a little more on weekends. A child who has a consistent routine can cope with change in a much more positive way. This means sleepovers, trips away, or overnight stays if you are seeing friends, should not impact on a child too much, if they have positive sleep patterns and associations in place the rest of the time.

Technology

If you allow your child screen time, ensure this is at least an hour and a half before bed (ideally 2-hours, although this may not be realistic).

Screens can affect sleep negatively in two ways. The first being the impact of the blue light source that is emitted, as this influences the production of melatonin, the sleep hormone and biologically keeps children from feeling tired (possibly why after lights out some children are still wide awake chatting). The second being the stimulating effect that screen time can have on the brain with exciting TV shows / gaming before bed, often leading to the release of hormones such as adrenaline, which can reduce the ability to fall asleep.

I do appreciate that many children enjoy television shows / gaming and I would not want to deprive them of this and can also appreciate how valuable it can be for parents to get crucial jobs done during this time! However, I would suggest that TV / screen time is allowed *before* children have their evening meal. If this is a new change that you are implementing, your child may be confused and make a fuss at first, but if you are consistent with your rules, they will learn to adapt to the change quickly.

If your child does not have a club after school, a general after school routine could consist of:

Snack / Screen time, homework, free-play, evening meal, wind-down time, bedtime routine, bed.

Diet

Try to not have the evening meal too late. It is important that children have sufficient time to digest their food before bed; eating late can have huge implications on sleep if the digestive system is busy working hard.

Puddings ideally should be a healthier snack, some fruit, nothing sugary and no chocolate (natural sugars only). If you do want your child to have special treats, think about allowing them something small straight after school so that the sugar intake does not impact sleep.

Tryptophan foods:

This may only be useful if your child greatly struggles with sleep and probably does not need to be amended if you only have minor concerns, however it is useful to be aware that some foods are actually 'sleep inducing foods'.

Foods which contain the amino acid 'tryptophan' can help boost the production of melatonin (the hormone that helps us sleep).

You can research foods that contain tryptophan, however common ones are chicken, turkey, milk, nuts and seeds - basically most protein rich foods. Ideally pairing these foods with a carbohydrate allows tryptophan to reach the brain more easily.

Bear in mind high-fat foods, sugary foods, spicy foods and food and drinks which contain small traces of caffeine, for example fizzy drinks, can keep children up at night - if your child loves these sorts of meals / drinks, try swapping them to lunchtime instead.

Homework

Try to ensure homework is not completed too close to bedtime. This can stimulate the brain and can cause some children to struggle with falling asleep. Homework can also often cause conflict at home - if this is the case for your family, remember, stress is not conducive to sleep.

As children progress through primary school, try and ensure there is a suitable place in the house where they can work. So many children tend to complete schoolwork sitting on their bed - a rule of thumb is that a child's bed should be purely for sleeping in, not working on - if a child consistently completes homework sitting on their bed, a 'bed association' develops that is not just related to sleep. Ideally, a table which is not in your child's room is best - but of course, if this is not practical, ensure there is a suitable desk / area in their room, away from their bed where they can complete their studies.

Exercise

Like many aspects of childhood this is about balance. A child who may not be very 'sporty' may need to have a brief walk after school in the fresh air to burn off energy and help them sleep better.

On the other hand, exercising too close to bedtime is also not ideal and this is important to consider when enrolling your child in clubs. Not only does your child not have sufficient time to unwind, but heat created by the muscles during exercise can prevent them falling asleep.

It is natural to sometimes want to tire your child out before bed, but it is a complete myth that if a child runs around or exercises at this time, they will be exhausted and sleep well - in fact, it has the opposite effect and wakes the body and mind up!

Time outside / fresh air

Having time outside in the fresh air positively affects the production of melatonin (sleep hormone). Try to consider the amount of time your child spends in the fresh air each day. On some days does your child have a snack or their evening meal in the garden? Do you encourage outdoor play? If you do not have a garden, do you walk back from school a few times a week? If there is a park you pass by, could you stop for a 15-minute play on the way home?

Fresh air is a free of charge resource and a little adaptation to ensure you squeeze it in after school, may make your life easier when it comes to bedtime!

Positive sleep hygiene, over time, can affect our sleep cycles, which should mean night waking will also decrease as a result, however the following points are useful to consider for children who may often wake during the night.

Night-time waking

If a child consistently wakes up in the middle of the night, or calls out to their parents, they are experiencing 'disturbed sleep'. Night-time waking can sometimes be a little harder to manage, partly because parents are exhausted and keen to want to return to sleep themselves.

Disturbed nights affect sleep cycles, therefore disrupt *meaningful* sleep. This will impact how a child feels the next day and thus, over time, affect a multitude of other childhood aspects.

Both children and adults sleep in cycles consisting of deep sleep and light sleep. A 'normal' adult sleep cycle lasts for about 90-minutes, whereas cycles are considerably shorter for babies and children, usually around 45 - 60-minutes. At the end of each cycle we all enter a stage of extremely light sleep and often wake up briefly during this time. Adults and children who have learnt how to sleep independently, just fall back to sleep straight away and are awake for such a brief amount of time, that they often do not even remember ever waking. However, those who have not learnt to self-settle and not learnt independent sleep associations, will often cry / call out at the end of some sleep cycles, as they need support to enter the next stage of their sleep - it is therefore fundamental to consider 'sleep associations'.

Sleep associations

One of the main reasons why children have difficulties in independently falling asleep, is because of the associations they have developed with night-time and falling asleep. We as adults also have these sleep associations; for example, some of us like to fall asleep watching television, listening to music, on a certain pillow, next to our partner, or even on a certain side of the bed! You may notice that when your main sleep association is removed, it is more difficult to fall asleep.

If, for example, a child falls asleep having their hand held or their parent sitting by their bed, it will be difficult for them to fall asleep again unaided when their sleep cycles naturally enter the lighter phase in the middle of the night. They will need their original environment in which they fell asleep to be recreated. Therefore, it is so important that your child is able to fall asleep independently at bedtime; this way they have a better chance of transitioning from one sleep cycle to the next during the night.

As parents, it is important to ensure that the sleep associations our children develop are appropriate for them as they grow up and mature (and appropriate and realistic for parents to maintain too). Sleeping with a certain pillow, toy, or comforter is an appropriate association, as it is sustainable, but requiring the constant presence of someone else is not. It becomes a huge strain on parents and also affects children as they grow up; the longer this association is embedded, the harder it is to make changes.

Often a child will wake or call out in the night if they have developed a 'parent-controlled sleep association'.

When a child develops a parent-controlled sleep association, then their strategies for falling asleep are completely dependent on *you*.

Parent-controlled sleep association examples:

- Stroking your child's hair or face until they fall asleep
- Holding your child until they fall asleep
- Sitting in your child's room until they fall asleep
- You sleeping in your child's bed
- Your child sleeping in your bed
- Reading to your child until they fall asleep

If you do believe your child has a parent-controlled sleep association, looking into ways to slowly change this reliance, over time, can greatly help with night waking. Even if your child does not wake in the night, but still has a parent-controlled sleep association, it is still useful to consider striving to adapt this before it becomes a habit and interferes with their independence and self-belief.

It is important that this is done over several weeks, so that it does not feel too much of a sudden change for your child.

To help with this you may like to consider:

- Leaving the room and offering your child 'check-ins' whereby you say goodnight and then return to check on them every 5-minutes. This way they will feel secure that you are still nearby. During the check-ins, make sure this is a brief look-in and not a full-blown conversation each time! As the days and weeks progress, increase the check-in time to every 10-minutes, then every 15-minutes and so on. You do not need to tell your child when you will be returning - just say 'very soon'.

- The gradual retreat approach is where you remain in your child's room, but slowly move your chair closer and closer to the door every couple of days. You then sit outside your child's room, then on the landing, then on the stairs, changing your location every two or three days, until you are permanently downstairs / away from your child's room. This approach takes a lot of patience from parents and should be done over a period of two - four weeks. It takes commitment and effort and can be incredibly frustrating sitting on a landing outside your child's bedroom door waiting for them to fall asleep. The long-term outcomes though can greatly help to reduce your child's anxieties and sleep dependence on you.

If your child does not have a parent-controlled sleep association, but still wakes in the night and experiences disturbed sleep, another idea (which I can appreciate may sound a little strange) is trying to manually adapt their sleep cycles. It is likely their sleep cycles may well have got into the pattern of waking at the same time each night. Monitor over a week or so, at what time this seems to be happening each night and see if there is a pattern. If there is, set your alarm for about 15 – 20-minutes before your child usually wakes up and calls out to you, go into their room, and gently rouse them. You should be waking them enough, so they stir, but not enough so they are wide awake and end up chatting.

This sometimes is enough to re-set your child's sleep cycles, so they do not wake up again that night. Try this for two weeks *consistently* to see if you can adjust their internal clock.

Sleep anxieties

It is common for children to experience extra anxiety at night-time, as this is the time that they are usually alone, able to focus on their thoughts and are not distracted by external people and stimuli. Their minds can wander, and they can develop patterns of worry and over-thinking. The 'dark' for some children can also add in extra concerns, especially for those who may be highly imaginative.

A consistent routine, *every day*, can help, over time, to greatly reduce anxieties, but our chapter 'General Worries and Anxieties' will explore how you can support your child with their concerns, without needing to seek Therapeutic support.

Points from our 'Encouraging Open Communication' chapter are also helpful here, in relation to sleep anxieties, as getting into a pattern of encouraging your child to regularly share their thoughts with you, can mean these do not build up during the day and surface at night.

Of course, always bear in mind that if your child is highly anxious and their long-term sleep patterns are seriously affected, you may need to seek help from a professional - the final chapter in this book will discuss this further.

Key 'takeaways' from this chapter to support positive mental health:

- ✓ Be aware of the fundamental impact sleep has on mental health and how it can influence so many different areas of life - both positively and negatively
- ✓ Assess if your child is regularly meeting the recommended number of hours sleep for their age

- ✓ Consider your child's sleep environment, routine and external factors / timings of activities which may influence their sleep patterns

- ✓ Consider introducing 'wind-down time' before bed, to encourage the production of the sleep-inducing hormone

- ✓ Be aware of your child's reliance on you when it comes to falling asleep and consider if this may need adjusting (especially as they mature)

CHAPTER SIX

Technological Usage

Therapeutic Goals to be considered at home:

· To try and understand further children's potential 'hidden communications' behind their technological usage

· To ensure appropriate limits are in place that children understand and feel content to follow, reducing potential screen time conflict within the home

· To develop an awareness around safety and age-appropriate play

How this builds Positive Mental Health:

· Supports a child in developing their self-awareness and understand further about the way they express their needs and respond to situations

· Helps a child grow up feeling secure with appropriate boundaries in place, responding appropriately to limits

· Reduces stress hormones in the body, in relation to conflict which may arise from disagreements around screen time

· Prevents a child experiencing increased anxiety due to engaging in inappropriate technological usage

Conversations around technology

For the sake of this chapter, the word 'technology' will be used to describe the use of any 'devices', such as mobile phones / tablets / iPads, as well as online gaming consoles, social media apps, and YouTube usage.

Technology plays a fundamental role in the western world with vast differences clearly apparent between how different generations grew up. Even if we examine the childhood of a young person today in their early teens, to the impending early years of a baby born this year, although theoretically these children would be classified as the same generation, advancements in technology and individual reliance on it have changed so much, even within a decade!

Every childhood event or milestone of our current generation is often captured via technology, ingraining into our children from their very first understanding of life the existence of technology. It is the world that they are growing up in and although this may be very different to how we, or our parents grew up, it is something that we have to consider carefully when raising emotionally healthy children in a technological-crazed society.

So, does technology within our homes actually affect the mental health of our children?

I am frequently contacted by families regarding this very question. Some examples of the nature of concerns that families have reached out to me about, and have been the driving force behind them accessing Therapeutic support for their child are:

- My child is addicted to gaming
- My child will not listen when I ask him to put down his screen
- Since getting a phone my daughter will not talk to me
- We have terrible arguments every day at home because I try to limit screen time
- My child saw something upsetting on YouTube and is now having nightmares
- My child is being bullied online
- Social Media is ruining my child's life
- My child is developing a poor body image because of the internet
- My child does not sleep well as they are always on their device

Creating positive and healthy behavioural patterns around technology, including appropriate boundaries as early as possible, is extremely important. Conflict at home can hugely influence well-being. For those who experience daily arguments, this, in fact is thought to cause a biological rise in the stress hormone, 'cortisol', in both adults and children.

This in turn can fundamentally affect overall mental health, as well as how our immune system operates.

Within this chapter, I will attempt to offer parents some thought provoking ideas around technology and the positive and detrimental effects of it. Technological battles feel a rite of passage that almost every parent will have to encompass at some point. The goal here being, to help you, as your child's first educator, to feel confident when dealing with technological issues within your home.

Our own behaviours and thoughts around technology

Something that I have observed, that is hugely important to initially consider as parents, is *your own* use of technology and phone time around your children. Perhaps stopping to think about what message this sends is worth contemplating, and how it may be affecting your child's developing relationship with technology, and thus their developing sense of self. In the early years, everything children observe, see, and hear has an impact on them and fundamentally this can play a huge role with regards to their behaviour as they enter the later stages of childhood.

If we grab our phone to capture everything our child does, are we teaching them technology is necessary to applaud their every achievement? If so, is it not then any wonder that for many children, technology might be rated as their number one choice of game or activity?

Your toddler takes their first steps, and you are desperate to share this with your family members who missed it; of course you are - it is probably one of their biggest achievements to date and you want others to enjoy this too. I am in no way suggesting that parents should not use their phones for these fundamental life milestones, however, perhaps consider celebrating *some* achievements without the aid of technology.

"We didn't have this in my day" is probably something every parent says, and probably something that every parents' parent said to them when growing up! The gulf between generations has always been there, but perhaps it is more distinctive today than ever, when extraordinary technological strides are occurring so rapidly. Expecting a child not to gravitate towards technology, because you did not have it when you were young, in some ways feels the same as expecting us as adults never to use the internet, because back in the day people would use encyclopaedias. Sometimes just amending our expectations and looking at them from other perspectives can alter how we feel, creating a more harmonious atmosphere at home.

Although of course there needs to be limits and boundaries around screen time, which we will explore, the critical point to first consider is:

How often does your child see you on your phone or device?

Understandably, many of us use our phones for work issues, banking, meetings, calls and generally organise the A to Z of our lives on them.

Let us stop a moment and think back to last week. What did you use your phone for that was not essential? What about when your children were with you? Did you still need to use it as much at the weekend when you had no work? Could you have used the time communicating with your children instead of scrolling?

This chapter is in no way a criticism whatsoever, but just a gentle reminder to be aware of our own use. If we are always on our devices, what message are we sending our children about technology?

Could this be the reason that when you ask your child to turn off their device, they may defy you or refuse, because what they see is you, constantly on your own device? It begs the question, can we expect our child to respect and listen to us about boundaries, if we do not follow them ourselves?

Can you recall a time that you were scrolling on your phone when your child was trying to talk to you? Could that be giving the message that your phone is more important than what they were trying to say? Children need to be heard and validated to feel a sense of self-worth.

I have lost count of the number of children who have said to me that mum / dad is always on their phone. When your child wants a chat, why not simply get into the habit of putting it down on the table or chair next to you, physically out of your hands. Listen to your child, then pick it up again once the conversation has ended, if you need to. This can be instrumental in ensuring a child leaves that conversation, knowing mum / dad felt it was important to fully listen to what they said, regardless of the topic. After all, if we do not listen to the 'small things' that our child shares, as per our 'Encouraging Open Communication' chapter, then why will they come to us with bigger, more worrying concerns down the line?

A few ideas you may like to consider with reference to your own use of technology within the home will follow. It is important to note that any changes will make no difference if they are carried out only *once.* The ideas are about amending our thoughts and actions slightly, which in turn can amend our long-term behaviours and create a positive home atmosphere, supporting our children in becoming emotionally healthy.

1. We often may pick up our phone or device using 'muscle memory', even if we have no reason to use it. Have you ever picked it up, swiped in your passcode and then wondered what you wanted to do? If you are watching a film with your children (however boring it may be) or playing a family board game, maybe try to keep your phone in another room to ensure your child sees your full focus is on

them and the joint activity. This removal of temptation may sound minor, but can go a long way in training our brains to lower our reliance on our devices. It also means that time with your child is not disrupted if you get a notification on your phone, that you are naturally eager to check.

2. Consider your use of photos and videos. How many times have I seen a child do something cute or funny and then hear their parent immediately say, "do that again!" as they grab their phone to capture the moment! Of course, do record your memories, whilst at the same time be mindful of *being in the moment* and enjoy your child's achievements with them in that instant, sometimes without a phone in your hand! Precious moments can be missed, and valuable opportunities lost to validate our children, when we are trying to save the moment via technology. To celebrate that special moment with your child, you could, (with younger children) sit down later and draw out the experience with them. Maybe they could draw a picture of them scoring that goal at football practise (the one you were so busy cheering for) and this could then be sent to a distant family member with a note from your child. The exercise itself of sitting down with a child and encouraging them to re-play out in their minds

something that made them feel personally proud, can be hugely beneficial.

3. Consider for a moment if you have ever actually asked your child if they want photos / videos taking. At one of their extra-curricular activities you may be on the sidelines filming every move to show a family member who could not make the event, but perhaps all your child sees is mum / dad using their phone. Check-in with your child, what would they like you to do? Would they prefer you cheering them on, phone in pocket instead? The more a child sees a parent valuing what they do or say, the more they will learn to value themselves!

4. If you have a photo that you love of your child that you want to send to a friend, or post on your own social media page, perhaps check-in with your child that you have their consent to do this? Even from a young age, a simple "Can I send this to Nanny?" is teaching a child about personal respect. Educating and demonstrating through your own behaviour, respect towards photos of your children, by the asking of permission and consent, can be fundamental in children learning key principles around photo sharing, safety, permission, and ownership - vital the older they get.

5. If you use public transport with your child and use your devices to track and check when the next bus / train is due, take a moment to guide your child on other ways they can do this. Help them to use the bus or train timetables displayed nearby. Teaching them non-technological reliance skills from a young age, can develop self-belief in themselves - another core principle of emotional health that we want to achieve.

Technological use as a communication

Now we have considered your own use of technology, your own behaviours, and the messages these may portray, we need to think of your children and their usage too.

Every behaviour is a form of communication, and sometimes what is difficult is endeavouring to see what is under the external presented behaviour. Perhaps we 'see' a child constantly on their device and arguing when we ask them to turn it off - but what is happening underneath this presented behaviour? Technological use can also be seen as a form of communication, just like any other form of play; of course you may feel that quite simply children just enjoy spending their time engaging in this sort of play, however often there is a reason behind it.

What are they getting out of it?

How is it making them feel?

Think again for a moment about your own desire and feelings behind your technological usage. Do you feel 'connected' with others when on social media? Do you feel a sense of 'achievement' if you play games online? Do you simply scroll on social media mindlessly to prevent thinking about everyday stressors? If you truly think about it, you may notice patterns; for example, if you have had a busy and happy week seeing family and friends in person, your social media usage could be lower, because you do not need to fill that void of feeling connected online. If you felt your performance at work was of a high standard, perhaps you may listen to music on the way home, instead of playing an online game, because you do not need that validation of feeling that you have done well at something. Whatever we all do, whether we are aware of the reasons behind it, or not, I can guarantee there is a reason and rationale behind every behaviour - in adults and in children.

There are ways, that you as parents can try to understand the inner world of your children, and so help to recognize further what your child may be feeling.

Through the following case studies, I hope you will be able to see that if we look a little more behind the presented behaviour, there may be further communications that are important to strive to understand. Moreover, through your understanding, this should help you to be guided on deciding the right technological limits to meet *your* child's emotional needs and so reduce conflict.

Case Study: Riley, aged 10

Riley came to Therapy for a number of different reasons, but in consultation with his mum, one of her main concerns was that Riley did not want to play outside anymore. He was always constantly wanting to 'game' upstairs in his room and would not show mum any respect when she asked him to stop playing. She was worried he was 'depressed' as he never had the motivation to do anything, except play on his device. Riley's mum also felt this was affecting his sleep and thus his mood levels the next day.

Within Therapy, Riley opened up about technology, his love and passion for his games and how it made him feel. Riley's parents were in the military and he had spent all his primary school years travelling and frequently changing schools. He liked this life and he liked exploring new places, but Riley really missed his friends and was beginning to find it hard to keep saying goodbye to them. It was through his gaming that Riley managed to maintain relationships with children he had met from previous schools. He could chat and type to them and it felt like he was with them. It was through regular sessions that Riley realised himself, that this was why he was always on his game and comprehended that how much missing his friends was affecting him and making him feel sad. He was able to eventually talk to mum about this, who was relieved to understand Riley's rationale, that he was not addicted to gaming, but that it was the only way he could independently maintain these vital connections. It also helped those around Riley realise how important it was for his mental health to have these consistent relationships with peers of his own age and how much he needed connections from his past to feel secure.

Through understanding Riley's individual relationship with technology further, Riley's mum was able to put in limits that he responded to better, whilst ensuring other ways of encouraging Riley to maintain connections with his peers. Feeling understood by others also helped Riley's moods. As Riley had always been keen to move and always said he liked his travelling lifestyle, it was of course hard for his family to see the impact that this was actually having on his health - Riley managed to hide this, and help his low mood through his technological use.

Case Study: Joshua aged 7

Joshua's mum arranged Therapy for him because she was worried about his behaviour - she explained he was often gaming with his friends and was worried this was making him 'aggressive'. Mum felt she had little control over the games he played at friends' houses and felt concerned that he had seen violent images online that were beyond his age.

She had observed Joshua hit his sister on multiple occasions, yet when she tried banning gaming at home, Joshua became unbelievably upset and aggressive and she did not know what to do. She was very worried the older he got, the more destructive his behaviour could become.

Many of Joshua's sessions within Therapy were very energetic and were based around play, rather than direct talking. Some of the play did involve certain fight scenes with toys, but what emerged with Joshua, was an internal feeling that he believed he was not very good at anything and always felt the need to ask for help, due to his own self-belief being low. Joshua felt he was terrible at football and PE and compared himself to the boys in his class who were always scoring goals. Joshua felt he was not very good at schoolwork either and he found things tricky, which made him feel angry at times. Joshua would compare himself to his sister, who was younger than him, but already better at certain subjects than he was. Something that Joshua felt he was very, very good at though, was battles! He would almost always beat his friends online at these and it made him feel amazing!

Joshua was actually struggling with quite low self-esteem, partly due to some mild learning difficulties, but also due to his constant internal comparison to peers in his school. Joshua's school was quite pressurised, and it was likely he had picked up on the importance of success early on, not helped by having a highly capable and over-achieving, younger sibling.

Gaming online was one of the few things that made Joshua feel good. It made him feel powerful and in control, when every day at school, he felt that everything was beyond his control. It also helped him to feel equal to his peers - they were good at sport and he was good at battles.

It appeared the hitting and anger at home, was not only some frustration towards his sister's capabilities, but a response to not feeling understood and feeling that the only thing he loved and was capable of, was being taken away from him. Through further understanding of Joshua's communications, we were able to think of other activities that Joshua could do, separate from school, to allow him the opportunity to develop skills and interests, which were individually suited to him, in order to help increase his self-esteem. Through his lack of confidence around sports, Joshua also had a lot of energy that he needed to expel. Joshua developed a sense of purpose, away from technology, through his new Taekwondo sessions, which involved a safe way of engaging in defence and attack 'battles'. Mum, in time, found home life became calmer and she was more confident in implementing boundaries, according to his needs.

Case Study: Emilie aged 11

Emilie's mum / dad initially requested for her to have some Therapeutic support because they said that since part-way through year 6, it felt like she had become a different child. They were worried that she was incredibly anxious about starting secondary school and explained that Emilie was rude at home and never wanted to do anything as a family anymore. She was always isolating herself in her bedroom and when asked to put her phone down or play a game with her siblings, Emilie would scream and shout.

Through regular sessions, it transpired that Emilie had always been a little girl who liked to please; she was always top of her class, well-liked by teachers and was always eager to help mum / dad at home. Emilie was given a phone during the middle of year 6, which she was happy about, but not over-excited. She preferred to play with toys and be creative instead. Within weeks though, she felt like her phone had taken over her life; multiple peer messaging groups were set up involving almost all her classmates and her friends would message her on them every night. Sometimes Emilie would switch on her phone after her evening meal to dozens of notifications of group messages. If Emilie did not reply, the next day she would go to school and felt her friends were mad at her. She felt like she had let them down and internally experienced an intense pressure to keep up with the constant influxes of messages, in order to prevent the unbearable feeling of being left out. She was stressed and overwhelmed, in fact actually disliked her phone, but the extreme peer pressure led her to feel it was easier to ignore her family and her siblings, than it was to ignore messages on her phone.

Part of the work with Emilie, especially as she entered secondary school, was helping her to understand her own desire to please others, whilst supporting her in understanding, accepting and prioritising her own needs too. Emilie felt an overwhelming pressure from peers, which then crept into her home life, when they were able to contact her out of school hours.

Peer pressure and technology is something I hear about frequently, but more often relating to older children and teenagers. It is something for all parents to be aware of though, in relation to *any* child who engages with technological devices that involve others at the same time. I have observed that peer pressure is not always direct. It does not have to be what we may view as 'cyber bullying', but can simply be peers putting pressure, without meaning to, on others, to *'stay longer and play'* or to *'not be a quitter'* if they have to log off. This is where differing boundaries between your home and your child's friends' homes can cause difficulties. I am sure it is likely you have heard, or will hear, something along the lines of "but my friends' parents let them play all the time!"

Unfortunately, Emilie is not alone with this feeling of technological pressure and this external, and internal strain to keep up with peers. This is something, that of course is prevalent in relation to overall school life and not just technology - however advancements in technology mean that children can now also communicate with peers *outside of school hours*, resulting in peer pressure that can be felt during the evenings, weekends and school holidays, not just in school.

The following points are helpful to consider in relation to peer pressure, although do not apply to bullying behaviours. Instead, they focus on milder, and common behaviours between friends, causing a child to feel an internal pressure to please via the usage of technology.

- Acknowledge how hard it may be for your child to say no to a friend or talk to them about their desire to please a friend. It is probably likely that if they are being told to stay and play for another game, they may find it easier letting you, as their parents down, knowing they are in a *safe place* at home, rather than letting a friend down.

- Peers are fundamental and vital connections for positive mental health, and it is no wonder that so many children value what their peers think and say so much. Finding a balance between limits, whilst respecting and encouraging suitable peer connections that your child has made is something to consider. It is important that you demonstrate to your child that you also understand and value how important their friendships are. When you demonstrate an understanding of this, children are far more likely to share how they may be feeling, or what their friend is saying to them, which will allow you to support them further.

The previous three case studies demonstrate that often there is some other form of communication behind a child's desire to continuously play on or use their technological device. These insights can stem from long-term Therapy work, and of course do not apply to all children. Nonetheless, they do demonstrate how important it is for parents to help their child feel more understood, improve parent-child connection, reduce conflict and therefore negative mental health effects.

Points for you to consider:

1. Having the notion in your mind that your child's frequent use of technology may be another form of hidden communication, is a great start. Just thinking about this may offer you some ideas as to why you feel your child may engage with certain technologies and what they may be internally gaining from it.

2. To understand the hidden communications further, try and show an interest and ask questions about your child's game / usage online - learn about what they are doing / how it works / how they may win or what they like about a particular YouTube

star. Showing an active interest enables parents to have access to what a child internally feels and thinks. As long as you are not showing any criticism towards their interests, you may be surprised how much children share with you and how much they enjoy mum / dad's curiosity in their favourite activity.

3. Sometimes writing things down can give more clarity than just thinking things through in your head. It is often in Therapy, that the notes written after a session, spike a resonance in a Therapist, who may then use that clarity in the following session to further support their work. Write down words your child may have shared (not when with them - we do not want them to feel they are being interrogated) and think things through a little more from their perspective, if possible.

4. Perhaps even have a game with your child on their device or console or sit and watch something with them that they love online. When doing so, be aware of your own feelings about what you may be experiencing, which may give you some further insight into what your child may be experiencing. Try hard to not share anything negative about the situation, even if you are not enjoying the game at

all; remember this is likely to be natural play for your child's generation. Demonstrating a dislike towards something your child loves, is probably not going to have any positive benefits down the line (although of course if their play or game is inappropriate, or unsafe, do express your concerns).

5. Do not be afraid to actually ask your child what it is that engages them and what their favourite part of their usage is (perhaps not when they are playing, as you may not get much focus from them, but at a later point in the day). Sometimes we avoid direct questions, but a child may give you a clear answer as to exactly what it is that they enjoy so much.

5. If you do get some further insight into your child's communication behind their usage, you can use this to consider carefully if there is anything else that could fill the void that technology is presently being used for. This may be initiating new interests or hobbies or alternatively it may be filled with increasing person-to-person connections, like additional one-to-one time with you, or more time spent socially with friends.

Imposing limits

It is now important to consider limits - whilst remembering your child is probably only going to respect your boundaries, if they do not see you constantly using devices yourself.

Why do we need limits?

It must be recognised that technology can have huge positive implications for children, not only during their childhood, but later in life too, in terms of skills developed which can support with technological jobs in the future. The negative effect of too much screen time, however, can be sleep disturbances, behaviour issues, weight gain, mood swings, lack of fresh air and lack of person-to-person communication, potentially even reducing family contact. Some thinking has also suggested that too much play via screens can reduce fine motor skills, as children are no longer spending as much time with construction toys, such as LEGO® or bricks, which help strengthen fine motor dexterity. Too much screen time can also distort a child's view of actual reality and affect their overall mental health when striving to cope with daily life.

I am not going to suggest how many hours a child should be allowed on screens each week. This is dependent on so many factors and circumstances that differ according to each family's unique set-up. It is up to you, as parents, to consider ways in which to create and maintain the limits in relation to your own family routine. It is important for your child to develop a positive understanding around the need for boundaries and regulations, which they will face throughout their life, even into adulthood - more on the overall importance of limits will be discussed later in our 'Healthy Boundaries' chapter.

You may like to consider the following to determine what feels appropriate for your own child, in terms of implementing technological boundaries within your home.

1. Think carefully when imposing time limits - for example, if you are allowing your child 45-minutes of screen time, it is likely you are going to have a situation on your hands if the game averages 55-minutes. Most children would struggle to stop part-way through a game. This could be because of their own feeling of dissatisfaction at not achieving, or peer pressure from those they may be playing with, who may see it as a travesty to leave a game unfinished. Chat to your child about what they plan to watch / play that day - perhaps find out how long a game, or show lasts, or when during the game, or show is a suitable time to stop. Can it be paused and carried on? Showing you care, shows your respect for *their* interests. Your child is far more likely to show that respect back to you, if you are working *together* with them to impose limits that feel fair for all.

2. Even if gaming or watching YouTube stars would be considered the worst way possible for *you* to spend 30-minutes of your free-time, showing an interest in what your child is doing can go a long way. Not only does it allow you to check out the levels of violence, child safety and security within the game (more about this later in the chapter), but it demonstrates to your child that you care and are keen to try something that appeals to them. Some children can find the transition between using their device and suddenly stopping at a set time, difficult. To support this, once their technology time has ended, you could enter into a discussion about their activity allowing them to share something funny or dramatic that may have happened! Allowing them a little discussion time about their usage once it is over can help with this transition away from technology and back to reality. It is common to ask our child every day about what they did at school, (with probably the majority saying 'nothing'), but if we expect to create a relationship centred around communicating, then encouraging your child to share things about the games and topics they may enjoy, is hugely important.

3. Probably something every parent has heard of is limiting screen time before bed. The biology behind this, as mentioned in our 'Developing Positive Sleep

Patterns' chapter, is that the blue light emitted from our devices affects the production of melatonin in our brains. Melatonin is the special hormone that tells our brains and bodies that we need sleep, so if this is not released appropriately, then it will be very hard for any child to fall asleep.

4. *Educate* your child on *why* you are imposing limits. You do not want to be seen as mum / dad just being difficult! Teach them about point three, in age-appropriate ways. Talk to them about your reasons and the effects of too much screen time. Sharing facts like this with a child, shows a mutual respect. Giving them the motivation and the responsibility to work out the limits with you, can make the task easier. Boundaries can help develop a positive sense of mental health. They help children accept important rules, feel secure, and give them a sense of ownership, especially when they can plan and monitor their own decisions alongside mum / dad.

Once you have put in place agreed limits, it is paramount to be as consistent as possible with these. If a child knows that they can manipulate mum / dad's rules, it is natural that they will strive to do so, which is when conflict occurs. If children are successful at manipulation once or twice, they will try, try and try again! They have seen they have done it before, so will believe they can do it again.

Monitoring technology outside of the home

This is something that is often beyond your control. Unfortunately, I have worked with many children who came to see me due to becoming incredibly anxious about certain characters or figures after playing an inappropriately aged game at a peer's house. Sharing with the parents of your child's friends the boundaries regarding technology, *you* have at *your house* is important. Some parents may let their primary school child play games which are rated 15, even 18, but you would hope, being aware of your rules, they would be vigilant when your child was having a playdate.

Ratings

It is up to every parent to decide whether they let their younger child play a game or view something that is rated above their years. I appreciate that this can be difficult especially when you have an older sibling in a house. I think it is very easy to underestimate the effect that these games have on a child, but from working with many children who have been effected by these (sometimes violent) action games via technology, the long-term goal is better to consider, rather than the short-term peace of giving in.

Long-term effects can be anxiety, insomnia, nightmares, the need for constant reassurance and, perhaps even professional support down the line.

I am in no way saying that every child who plays a 15 or 18 rated game or views a film classified above their age, will be negatively effected and need external support, but the simple fact of the matter is that you just do not know if your child will be impacted. Children in early primary school often do not have the capacity to distinguish between reality and fantasy and for them the character on YouTube that popped up on their screen one day, is in fact very, very real. You may feel that developmentally, because of their age, your child has grown out of this, but some children can live in the world of fantasy for longer periods of time than others. They so want to believe in the good and exciting world that can revolve around Unicorns, Father Christmas and the Tooth Fairy, enthusiastically enjoying this make-believe world throughout primary school. However, this can translate into other areas too - if Santa can visit all the houses on Earth in one night, then of course it makes sense to some children, that a scary figure in a game could touch their lives too.

If your child has seen something online that has scared them, listen carefully to their worries and continue to offer them support and reassurance. It is not helpful to belittle their feelings or tell them not to be silly. There will be more discussed in relation to this, in the chapter 'General Worries and Anxieties'.

Should their anxiety persist, you may wish to try one of the following:

Draw on paper or model the character with playdough or clay, then change it with your child to represent it as a funny and silly persona instead. Add colourful feathers coming out of the nose, a big lipstick cheesy smile or pom-pom cheeks etc. The exercise should be done together and should involve lots of laughter - no idea is too silly! The aim of this is to help your child envisage the character in a different way and to imagine this 'image' when worrying thoughts come into their mind.

Often even programmes / characters produced for children on TV or in films, can evoke fear. Something that can help here, is showing children the real-life actor, behind the make-up, and explaining to your child how it is clever face paint and styling that makes them look the way they do. Try to find the real-life actor in the happiest of photos, looking friendly, or having fun. This should help your child distinguish further between reality and the make-believe figure.

Technological safety

Most parents are probably aware of parental controls and locks that you can install on your devices to ensure that what your child is independently participating in, is safe and suitable for their age. I have worked with countless children who have observed something inappropriate online whilst briefly using their parents' device. Bear this in mind with *all* the devices in your house - a child does not have to actively search for something for 'pop-ups' to appear.

It is important to also be aware of technology that allows children to play or chat with others at the same time. If this is with their peers, or classmates, it can help to cement friendships out of school and can be a positive experience, but always be mindful and check who your child is engaging with online. By showing an interest, you can find this out discretely, without making it obvious you are checking up on them. Children are never too young to be educated about the importance of online safety. Reinforcing this during the primary school years is so important for ensuring a clear level of understanding when children reach secondary school and become more technologically independent. With the swift advancement of technology be sure to keep fully informed on the guidance given by the Government via the UK Council of Child Internet Safety on how to keep your child safe online.

Key 'takeaways' from this chapter to support positive mental health:

- ✓ Consider your own use of, or reliance on technology and the message this may be portraying to your child

- ✓ Be aware that extensive usage of devices can sometimes be a hidden communication of a child's need

- ✓ Consider your child's screen time limits and the ways in which these are imposed, in order to reduce stress and conflict

- ✓ Be aware of technological safety, your child's use of technology outside of the home and game / film ratings and how these can impact anxiety and mental health

CHAPTER SEVEN

Healthy Boundaries

Therapeutic Goals to be considered at home:

· Helping children understand the need for and the importance of boundaries, allowing them to develop an understanding of safe and appropriate limits

· To ensure children know what to expect at home, allowing their voice and opinions to be heard, whilst feeling content that the adults around them are responsible for key decisions

How this builds Positive Mental Health:

· Helps a child feel secure, whilst reducing stress, anxiety and uncertainty and developing trusting relationships with those around them

· Helps a child feel heard, validated, and listened to

· Supports a child in understanding and managing societal expectations, as well as developing personal boundaries and self-respect in relation to others

We have discussed implementing specific boundaries at home in terms of technological usage and bedtime / sleep routines, however it is also very important to consider further boundaries relating to everyday aspects of childhood and family life.

Quite simply, boundaries are fundamental in supporting and maintaining your child's mental health. Without clear guidance, rules, limits, and expectations children can lose their way, negatively impacting their external relationships, as well as their overall sense of self. A relationship without limits, be that a parent-to-child relationship, or a peer-to-peer relationship, has little value in terms of mutual respect.

So why are boundaries important?

1. Boundaries help children develop a sense of security, knowing what to expect from those around them. This security helps children develop a feeling of trust, building resilience and reducing anxiety.

2. Clear and consistent boundaries can reduce conflict and stress, two facets not conducive to positive mental health.

3. Boundaries help children learn to manage, cope, and succeed in aspects of life, away from home, whilst encouraging children in learning self-control and making healthy and safe choices independently.

4. Boundaries help children to develop personal respect and an understanding of how they expect to be treated by others.

It is so common for many parents to sometimes want to be lenient with their boundaries at home, for fear of not wanting to be viewed by their child as 'too strict'. They feel they want to allow their child freedom and independence to be who they want to be. Although this is also important for children's development, I hope this brief chapter will offer some ideas for parents to comprehend that boundaries at home can be healthy and can be achieved in a positive way, strengthening your relationship with your child.

Just as the existence of boundaries is important, the way the boundaries are imposed with kindness and in a clear and loving way, is also just as important and will also be explored within this chapter. First, perhaps consider these questions and jot the answers down on the 'Notes' section at the back of the book, if need be:

1. What boundaries do we have at home?
2. Are we consistent with our boundaries?
3. Does my child understand the boundaries?

4. Are there any more boundaries that would be useful to consider?

Examples of boundaries within the home environment

A boundary that is suitable for one family, may not work for another, therefore it is not possible to say which boundaries should be imposed; each family dynamic is different.

Listed are a few questions to consider when thinking of your own home limits. It does not mean you need specific rules in every area described, but the examples are aimed to help pinpoint what we mean when we use the word 'boundary.'

Technology / screen time

Do you have set rules in place, or time limits for technology / screen time? Do you monitor your child's activities when using technology? Are there certain days, or times that screen time is limited? What are the rules when siblings, or other family members want to play / use the same device?

Sleep and the bedtime routine

Do you have set bedtimes? Is there clear guidance about what is allowed and when, in the run up to bedtime? Does your child dictate their own bedtime and independently take themselves to sleep? Are there rules for siblings who share a bedroom? Can your child eat snacks before bed?

Free-time

What is allowed during free-time? Are children allowed in your room? Are they allowed on your devices, or access items belonging to mum / dad? Does your child need to ask to get out certain activities, or can they play with anything they like?

Tidying up after themselves

Does your child have rules on this, or do you tidy up after them? Are there limits on making a mess?

Independence

Can your child play out on the street? Can they independently take their bike out? Do they always need to be with mum / dad when not in the house?

Personal space

Are there boundaries around personal space in your home? Do you have locks on the bathroom doors? Does your child have their own space to go to for some quiet time? Do they respect your quiet space?

Work

If you must work from home, or make a personal call, do your children have boundaries in place to respect this time and engage in quieter activities? Is there an office in your house that children know not to enter?

Siblings

Do siblings have their own privacy / personal belongings, or is it a 'free for all' situation? Do siblings have to knock when they enter each other's bedroom? Do you have rules on sharing? Are siblings allowed to express their feelings physically to one another?

Food

Are your children allowed the freedom of snacks whenever they want? Is chocolate allowed before mealtimes?

Safety

Can they cross the street on their own, or do they hold your hand? Are there boundaries regarding speaking to strangers, or clear restrictions on sharing personal information online?

When analysing home environments, there are probably so many more questions that we can think of in terms of boundaries, but the previous ideas offer some thinking points with regards to your own home life.

Perhaps you are a family who is very rigid in terms of food and healthy eating, but more flexible in terms of free-time and what your child can select to do. However you work as a family, it is fundamental that the boundaries you choose to initiate at home, are *consistent.*

Pushing boundaries and consistency

It is natural and healthy for young children to push boundaries; this is how they learn. Children need to push and test in order to understand what is acceptable and what is not. This is also how they learn about those around them - *who* is consistent and trustworthy, and who is not. It is important to accept the pushing of boundaries as a crucial part of childhood. Your child is usually not trying to be difficult, but they are figuring out their own power and impact on the world. We will explore this more at the end of the chapter.

If you are inconsistent with your boundaries, for example, five times a week you stick to your limits and say 'no' to something, and two times a week (perhaps because you are tired or frustrated with their constant demands) you give in and agree, then your child will continue relentlessly, to challenge you. Not only that, but it is likely to trickle in and affect other boundaries that you have in place and this can cause stress and conflict. Over long periods of time, it can also cause some difficulty around trust - how is a child meant to trust what someone says, if they keep changing their mind? Forming trusting relationships is a big part of positive mental health.

If you are consistent with your limits, a child will probably still initially try and push them, but after time will realise mum / dad is not budging and this will cease.

Besides conflict, this power play around boundaries can have a far more negative impact on your child's developing sense of self, than just some frustrating family arguments. When a child feels in control over certain rules or decisions at home, the balance of power shifts towards the child. When a child internally feels that they can convince mum / dad to agree to whatever they want, it is likely the child develops a feeling of being more powerful at home, than his or her parents. This feeling of being able to control a person - who should be in charge - can in fact make a child feel anxious, long-term. Although they may get immediate gratification by obtaining what they want, over a prolonged period of time, this uncertainty can negatively impact overall mental health.

Continued, lack of boundaries and consistency can also affect children's relationships with others. Positive relationships with family members and those outside of the home, are imperative for mental health, yet when these develop inappropriately or are impacted negatively, this can also affect how emotionally healthy your child feels.

It is very common for a child with inconsistent boundaries, or no boundaries, to either present in an overly cautious manner, for fear of not wanting to get something wrong, or, display the complete opposite attitude and act in an unruly fashion, as a way of striving to figure out where the boundaries lie. Both types of behaviours are understandable if what was allowed yesterday, is not allowed today.

Case Study: Darcie aged 9

Darcie came to Therapy due to consistent difficulties at school. She struggled to follow instructions and was often sent out of class due to being rude to her teacher. Darcie struggled with any form of team game or activity and would over-rule many of her peers when it came to making decisions. As a result, many of her classmates would keep their distance and Darcie found playtimes difficult. She would often complain to teachers that other children were unkind and leaving her out. Darcie would come home after most school days very low and emotional, feeling she had no friends. Darcie's parents tried to enrol her in external clubs, but she continued to be adamant, saying that others did not treat her well. The school and Darcie's parents were considering whether Darcie may have a form of mild autism, due to her difficulties engaging socially with others.

After regular Therapy sessions, and Darcie striving to break and cross all the boundaries of the Therapy room, it appeared what Darcie needed was consistency and clear expectations. Due to naturally being quite an assertive child, and an only child, it was often easier for Darcie's parents to let her dictate many of the family decisions at home. This would stop arguments and appeared to keep Darcie happy (which was understandably important to mum / dad, especially as Darcie appeared so unhappy coming home from school each day).

On meeting Darcie, she seemed a very confident child. She was vocal and happy to assert her views and opinions. She presented as a child with high self-belief and self-esteem. However, Darcie was really struggling within. Darcie had developed, over time, patterns of self-absorption - which may sometimes look like confidence and high self-esteem, but is in fact different. Darcie found it hard to create positive relationships with those around her which were not based on fulfilling her own wants and needs. She could not understand why others did not listen to her and play the games *she* wanted. It became more and more difficult for her. Her only understanding of this, was that her peers did not like her, and as a result her self-esteem became very low.

Over time, and with support, Darcie's parents felt confident enough to slowly begin to impose certain boundaries at home. Naturally, this evoked many household arguments, but by keeping to their word and being consistent, the power balance at home changed. This in turn affected Darcie's power balance at school. She slowly learnt, with support, that her peers were equal to her and entitled to their own opinions and views.

In essence, as much as children need opportunities to assert themselves and their opinions (we will explore this later), a parent must be the overall frontrunner. This is not to be unkind, or assert age over a child, but it is for the general long-term benefit of them. Boundaries ensure relationships feel mutual, respectful, appropriate, and enjoyable, both in and out of the home environment. Darcie's relationships initially did not possess any of these qualities, affecting her mental health and sense of self in many ways.

Darcie also struggled with listening and responding to her teachers' requests, another aspect of the importance of boundaries. If a child pushes the boundaries within the home, due to inconsistencies and knowing they are likely to 'win', then of course they will push these when away from home, in school, or extra-curricular settings. This can not only cause conflict and negative relationships with these adults but can also impact a child's academia and enjoyment of activities, if most of their time is spent pushing and testing the boundaries.

Simply put, boundaries are important for society. If a child cannot function appropriately in everyday society, then this can greatly impact them.

Personal boundaries

Understanding that boundaries exist, help a child to comprehend that rules also relate to their own lives in one way or another and helps them determine in what ways they expect to be treated by others. This notion of self-respect is an important aspect of positive mental health, as with self-assurance comes the knowledge of knowing what is right and wrong. A child with little, or no boundaries, may think it is OK for another child to bully them, because for them, limits are confusing and hazy. Some teenagers who have very few boundaries when it comes to their own personal respect, will allow others to treat them inappropriately, due to not feeling able to impose their own personal limits.

If your teenager had consistent boundaries within their primary school years, this is likely to make your life much easier as they enter secondary school, when you will of course have to amend limits appropriately.

Involving children in decisions

When it comes to boundaries, taking your child's view and voice into consideration is important. When children's opinions are taken notice of, they are often much more motivated to follow the rules and to co-operate. This also makes them feel respected.

Primary school children, even in early 'reception' years, are of an age when they can understand and make agreements about what is acceptable and what is not. They are also of an age when they can suggest and share their insights too.

An idea to support this, is having written 'Family Rules', or a 'Family Contract'. It is completely up to you what you call it - you may be opposed to the word rules, or contract, although I have found some children like the idea of calling it the latter, as a 'contract' feels official and mature.

If you feel you are lacking boundaries at home, then this is a helpful way to begin. The discussion can be calm, kind and fair - it does not have to be about being strict or assertive, but simply sharing appropriate guidelines.

· Initiate a family meeting, with all involved, who live in the house.

· Think carefully about the time you do this, i.e. not after a stressful day, not in the evening when people are tired, and not when you need to rush out the door. It does not have to be formal - you can even enjoy some snacks during it!

· Ideally sit around a table, so all involved can visually see each other - this is important, so all feel heard.

· Explain that it is important everyone listens to each other and nobody interrupts.

· If you are using the word 'contract', explain what this means, in age-appropriate ways.

· Explain that the meeting is about your special family rules / limits / boundaries - whatever you choose to call them. Make it clear why you need these - to keep us safe / for things to feel fair / so we know what to expect / so we do not argue about silly things etc. Children need to know *why* rules are being imposed, so they understand why they should be followed.

· As the adult, start by writing down a few things that you feel are important (if you are in a two-parent family, make sure you discuss this before, as it is very important children see parents in agreement together).

· Offer each child in the house an opportunity to contribute. This can be extremely valuable and allows children the time to share things that they feel are bothering them. For example, a sister may want her brother to knock before he goes into her room. Sorting issues like this out altogether, can make home life more harmonious.

· If your children's requests are reasonable and manageable, add them into the contract. "I want sweets every day" would not be considered an appropriate 'boundary' to add!

· Go through the final list and ensure everyone is happy. For younger children who cannot yet read, you may want to add some visual pictures to represent the boundary.

· Ensure there are not too many boundaries listed, as this can feel overwhelming. Eight to ten should probably suffice. Of course, there will be other boundaries at home that are not listed, but write down the most relevant ones, unique to your family dynamics.

· Allow all to sign or write their name at the end. Younger children may like to colour or decorate it too.

· Display this in a commonly used family room - the kitchen is usually ideal - for all to see.

· Remind children of the contract, either by pointing to it, or naming it, as and when appropriate. This can be helpful to ensure you are consistent and to ensure the way you enforce these guidelines feels fair.

If you do not feel a family meeting, or contract is appropriate for your family dynamics, then boundaries are still important to be considered using the following points:

· Ensure appropriate and suitable boundaries are in place.

· Ensure these are followed and as parents you are consistent.

· Ensure children are aware of these boundaries.

· Ensure children's views and opinions are taken into consideration.

As children grow and develop, certain boundaries naturally change. Always explain any amendments and the reason for them. This helps keep the consistency, but maintains the feeling of security and the understanding not to push the remaining boundaries.

Special occasions

Although consistency is imperative, it is important to distinguish the difference between 'consistency' and 'special treats'. If there is a rationale behind amending your boundary slightly, such as a very special event, a birthday or a sleepover, children must still see that mum / dad are consistent the rest of the time. Boundaries are not there to stop enjoyment, but be clear with your child that the 'special treat' is a one-off.

Just remember, that it is easy for one-offs to turn into regular occurrences, so continue to be consistent and stand your ground in the future - remembering it is for the benefit of your child, long-term!

What to do when my child pushes the limits

As we mentioned earlier, it is natural for children to try and push limits and even with a beautifully drawn up family contract, boundaries will still at times, be challenged. How you manage this, however, sets a precedent for the future, as well as offering your child invaluable life lessons and self-awareness development.

I am sure if you spend a couple of moments, you can think of a time when your child was being obstinate - they were provoking you, on the verge of what seemed as threatening, implying that they were about to do something that was not permitted! Your most natural response in the heat of the moment, would probably have been to shout "no!" and become annoyed, or rush over in anger to stop your child's actions. However, this is not always helpful. If possible, in these circumstances, practise getting into the habit of relaying the boundary back to your child in a clear, calm, patient way. Try not to appear rushed or panicked, as this shows lack of trust that your child will make the correct decision.

Let us imagine a scenario where your child may be goading you that they are going to eat a sweet just before lunch which they know they are not allowed. It might feel easy to quickly pull the sweet out of their hand, but what is that teaching them? Possibly, that you do not trust them to do the right thing. Instead, by remaining calm, and with careful use of your words and actions you have a valuable opportunity to demonstrate your faith in your child's decision. This belief can go a long way in raising an emotionally healthy child, who has their own internal self-belief system too.

In a situation like this:

- Acknowledge your child's feeling / need
- Be clear on the limit
- Suggest alternatives

"Yes, I know that you really want to eat that sweet but not before lunch. You can put it here and you can have it after we have eaten."

Showing empathy to a child's initial desire can diffuse the situation far quicker, than engaging your initial instincts to shout and take the sweet away.

Let us look at a few more examples:

"I can see you are angry with me right now. We do not hit people. You can hit the pillow if you need to get out some of your angry feelings."

"I know you want to go on your iPad while you eat. We do not have any screens when eating. You can put it on the side for when you are finished."

"I can understand that you really want to play with your brother's ball. You do not take his things without asking first. You can ask him when you can play with it."

With all these phrases, you are *validating* a need or a feeling, being very *clear* and *consistent* with the boundary, but offering an *alternative*. You are giving your child a *choice* whether they want to act on their original impulse or try and engage with the new suggested behaviour. You are offering an opportunity for your child to make a *positive decision* independently.

Positive life choices are fundamental for positive mental health. Installing self-belief in independent decision making during primary school, is vital for the teenage years, when opportunities for unsafe or inappropriate decision making, will likely present itself.

I appreciate that it may take a little bit of time to get into the pattern of responding to your child like this. Staying calm really is the key - perhaps try this method a few times and see how your child reacts.

Key 'takeaways' from this chapter to support positive mental health:

- ✓ Remember that boundaries are needed. They are not there because you are being strict or unkind. They are necessary and vital for your child's development - healthy boundaries are in place to make sure your child maintains positive mental health

- ✓ Consider your family's boundaries in and out of the home, ensuring these are consistent, your child is aware of them and that their views are taken into consideration

- ✓ Consider calm ways to respond when your child pushes boundaries, encouraging positive decision making skills and a demonstration of trust in your child

- ✓ Monitor the power balance in your household, ensuring it is the adults who make the key decisions within the home

CHAPTER EIGHT

Making Mistakes, Failing and Coping When Things Go Wrong

Therapeutic Goals to be considered at home:

· Supporting children to accept and move on from mistakes, failing and things going wrong

· Ensuring children do not internalise mistakes as a representation of who they are, thus affecting their self-esteem

· Helping children to develop a 'growth mindset'

How this builds Positive Mental Health:

· Helps to build a child's resilience, enabling them to cope and bounce back from difficult times

· Helps to build a child's self-belief and identity awareness, not just based on achievements and successes

· Helps to encourage a positive mindset which can be applied to multiple areas of a child's life

Mistakes, failings, and things going 'wrong' are a fundamental part of daily life for everyone, both adults and children, enabling us to learn, grow and develop, so progressing through life in a positive way. What is very important to consider, is not the actual mistakes and failings themselves, but the way we manage the repercussions of them. How do we cope? How do we move on?

Before we can even consider moving on, the first thing we all must be able to do, is accept what we have done or what has happened. It is not possible to move on from anything if we cannot accept the mistake or feeling of failure in the first place. Acceptance leads to management of the situation which in time, allows us to hopefully learn from the experience and either:

1. Try not to repeat the same mistakes
2. If we do, cope better with the effects of them and learn from them

Often feelings around mistakes and failings and our acceptance of them, are routed in our own personal expectations of ourselves and the expectations of those around us. Something that may be thought of as a failure, or catastrophic error to one person, may feel minor, or insignificant to another. Person A may be able to deal with a spelling mistake on a piece of homework or work presentation and move on, but person B may not be able to cope, and may have to spend time re-writing and checking the entire piece of work again. This is likely due to persons A and B having very different expectations. Children's expectations of themselves, are often rooted in the expectations that their parents have of them.

The word mistake, or failure can have many negative connotations, and is more often associated with adults; after all, how often does a young child really 'fail' or make a serious 'mistake'? For a child of primary school age, this vocabulary does seem rather strong, but could be considered in terms of the following:

· Losing a game

· Failing a test at school

· Not being picked for a sports team

· Not scoring any goals in a match

· Making an error on a piece of homework

· Missing a deadline for a piece of homework

· Spilling something and ruining a carpet

To us, in the adult world, with our responsibilities and constant everyday demands, these small mistakes and failings may seem minor. As a result, it can be natural to expect a child to pick themselves up and carry on. However, it is important to remember that for a child who has yet to experience and understand the complex adult world, these factors often feel huge. Sometimes it can be helpful for us as parents to put this into perspective. Failing a weekly spelling test to a child, may be similar to your feelings if you have missed a deadline and let your boss down. Not being picked for a sports team for a child, may be as disappointing as you not receiving the promotion that you worked so hard for.

The way in which a child learns to cope with mistakes and failures is an integral part of developing positive mental health. Responses to these sorts of situations, that will naturally crop up in everyday life, help shape who your child will become as a person and is a fundamental part of developing resilience. A child who is consistently reprimanded and blamed for errors, misjudgements and failures is likely to not only shy away from opportunities in the future, but may in time display low self-esteem and self-belief. As we have seen in previous chapters, this then could start to affect wider areas of a child's life, for example, their relationships with others, causing possible further mental health decline. It is important, as parents, to monitor our own expectations of our children.

It is easy for external mistakes to be translated into internal feelings.

"I did not do well on that maths test, that means I am not very good with numbers"

"I lost the game, I lose everything, I am useless at everything"

Mistakes and failures left or encouraged to fester and grow in a child's mind, can diminish confidence and manifest in their behaviours. For example, if they are constantly worrying that they will do or say something wrong, they can start to overthink social situations and everyday interactions can become highly stressful. A child can become worried that they will make 'mistakes' and be judged in a poor light by their peers.

"I said something really stupid to Maggie - Maggie thinks I am stupid - I am stupid - everyone thinks I am stupid"

Unfortunately, these thought processes and behaviours can become habitual in a child, if they are not taught how to manage and deal with their own occasional failings, mistakes and misjudgements. (We have discussed how behaviours can become a pattern, in our 'Expressing Feelings and Emotions' chapter). One of the key goals to remember here, is that to raise an emotionally healthy child is to raise a resilient child. Resilience has been mentioned frequently within this book and is integral to our mental health; resilience is quite simply the ability to cope with stress, failure, challenges and even traumas and is a skill that is developed throughout childhood, through nurturing and appropriate parenting. A child who has not developed positive resilience skills will struggle greatly in many situations.

We often describe one strand of positive mental health as the 'ability to bounce back from tough times', but if a child cannot bounce back from a small wrongdoing or failure, how then will they be able bounce back from something that may have a much larger impact on their life?

A child's internal struggle to cope with mistakes, or things going wrong, can in time influence their sense of self, their self-esteem, their peer relationships, their academia, and their overall general well-being. For some children, initial difficulties around accepting mistakes and failures can turn into an unhealthy association with 'perfectionism', and a desire for everything they do to be 'perfect', or to be *seen* as 'perfect'. Their lives then become a constant struggle trying to achieve something that is very often unattainable. For teenagers in secondary school, I have seen this develop into body image concerns, and more harmful behaviours.

As parents it is important for us to support our children when things go wrong, and to help them grow up in an environment where mistakes and failures are learnt from and are not viewed as disastrous. Please however do not be too concerned if your child is already displaying worries over these, as there are still many ways to support them, which we will discuss in this chapter.

Let us look at the examples of Liliana and Louis.

Case Study: Liliana aged 8

Liliana experiences great internal pressure every day to be the 'best'. She tries incredibly hard in all her work, her home studies and her sports and is a high achiever. However, for Liliana, despite being so young, if she is not the top of the class, or the highest goal scorer, she sees this as a 'failure' and will only display positivity towards her performance, if she is better than everyone else. Her parents only celebrate her achievements if they are one hundred percent. If she does not meet their high expectations, she is questioned on the reason for not being the 'top' of the class or the 'best' in the team and is asked endlessly how she intends to better the result. This causes Liliana further stress as she is constantly pushing herself to practise her sports and spends a considerable amount of time 'revising' for minor assessments / quizzes at school. This idea of needing to be the best, is translating into her peer relationships and if a friend chooses not to play with her, she assumes this is because she is 'not good enough'. Liliana is constantly coming home convinced her friends do not like her. Her self-esteem is fragile and based around achievements and external validation from peers.

Rather than feeling resilient to cope with difficult situations, Liliana has internalised external 'failures' onto herself, which are now being translated beyond academia, affecting her peer relationships. Liliana has a view that she is only 'good' if she succeeds and bases her feelings of self-worth on achievements, rather than her own personality and unique qualities. Liliana needed support in adjusting her mindset, developing resilience skills and some further empathetic understanding around peers. She needed to comprehend that they may choose to play with others for multiple reasons, that are not based around her accomplishments. It was also important for Liliana's parents to become further aware of their own expectations. Although they only had good intentions in wanting their daughter to succeed to the best of her abilities, they needed to also show Liliana that not always achieving one hundred percent was OK and was not a reflection on who she was as a person.

Case Study: Louis aged 11

Louis could not bear to lose any game, even a board game, and would often have extensive tantrums, even when on the edge of losing. Louis has always struggled with this, but it escalated when it came to any interaction or play with his older brother, whom Louis compares himself constantly to. From Louis's perspective, his brother can do anything; he achieves well at school, he is captain of the rugby team, he has many friends and he never seems to struggle. Louis views his brother as 'perfect' and strives to be the same. He will spend hours re-writing out homework just so it is 'neat' and seen as 'perfect'. His parents constantly praise his brother and ask Louis why he does not do so well. His brother gets rewards and Louis often has to stand by and watch. More recently, Louis has begun washing his hands multiple times a day, to the point his knuckles are now red and visibly sore. Louis does this as a way of maintaining control and to exert his internal feelings of wanting things to be 'perfect' by ensuring high levels of cleanliness.

Washing hands is frequently viewed as OCD (Obsessive Compulsive Disorder), however there are many aspects that contribute to a diagnosis of this kind. In this case Louis did not have diagnosable OCD, but was displaying 'OCD tendencies'. Having an over-achieving sibling can be difficult for many to manage. On top of his parents overwhelming pride in his brother, Louis was never able to forget all the mistakes he made in tests, homework, and his failure in sports achievements because he was reminded of them repeatedly. Similar to Liliana, Louis needed support to understand winning and losing was not an interpretation of who he was as a person. He needed support to see his uniqueness and self-worth, separate to his brother.

Internal pressure around schoolwork, sports, lack of enjoyment surrounding non-competitive games and impacted peer relationships are all common signs of a child who may be struggling internally with mistakes and failures. The secondary school years are often a time when young people are finding their identity and the workload and peer competitiveness increases, often causing a sharp rise in stress levels. Inevitably, mistakes will be made, and things will not always go as planned. It is important a teenager can accept and move on from their mistakes, lapses in judgements and cope with feelings of dissatisfaction. Commonly I have seen children in early secondary school displaying harm towards themselves, as a form of 'punishment' for something that they felt they did 'wrong'. Setting your child up with resilience skills now, *before* secondary school, will go a long way.

How do *you* as parents cope with mistakes and failings?

It is important, as parents, to evaluate your *own* behaviours in relation to the mistakes and failures that are naturally a part of your life too. In early childhood, children mirror so much of what they see and hear around them. The more they see their parents dealing positively with something that went wrong, the more they will develop skills to do the same themselves. Perhaps spend a few moments considering how you feel when you make a mistake.

Are you able to accept it, move on and try again, or does it impact you for some time?

Do you have sleepless nights over things which may have gone wrong? Is this clear for others to see?

Being aware of your own behaviours is an integral first step.

Sharing mistakes that you may make, out loud, to your children, can be very helpful. If you have burnt the evening meal, taken the wrong turn on a road trip, or if something went wrong at work, do not always feel the need to hide this from your children. Sometimes sharing these, in age-appropriate ways, can be instrumental in teaching your child how to cope themselves.

As we mentioned in the 'Expressing Feelings and Emotions' chapter, allowing your child to hear you say sorry, or show remorse if need be, demonstrates that you make mistakes too, but are able to accept them, respond appropriately and move on. Children need to know that mistakes are a part of life, even for adults. It is natural for us to want our children to view us in certain ways or protect them from certain experiences. However actually, if we are unconsciously hiding our own mistakes and failures from them, this can create an ideology for children that mum / dad are perfect and that they too should strive to be 'perfect'. It also is likely, they might not come to you for help if they have made a mistake, especially the older they get, as they may feel you would not understand. Viewing your own mistakes as healthy, actually helps create healthy children.

Be aware of the language you use when you critique yourself and your mistakes in front of your child. Try not to use negative language about yourself such as 'stupid'. A young child can then mimic this language when faced with their own mistake or failure, proceed to internalise this, and begin to actually feel they are 'stupid'. The important goal for our children, is that mistakes, failures and misjudgements are *never* internalised, resulting in a negative belief in themselves. Children need to understand and distinguish the difference between a behaviour, and who they are as a person.

Whilst on the subject of criticising yourself in front of your child for your errors of judgement, mistakes and failures, I would just like to add here that it is important to be careful on weight issues and food. Your child may hear you constantly say that you should not have eaten that chocolate bar, had that second portion in the restaurant or even that you 'failed' to lose the two pounds you were aiming for this week. A young child may grow up believing these were 'mistakes' on your part and as a result start unconsciously emulating what you did to rectify them. It can be the start of the idea of 'perfectionism' which many children develop from a very young age when they cannot manage failures appropriately. This can of course lead down a very sad path towards harmful behaviours later in life. Although it is easy to feel this may relate more to older children and teenagers, it is very, very important to remember that many teenage behaviours stem from early childhood experiences. It is also imperative to note, this relates to boys too - with many boys, not just girls, experiencing difficulties around body image.

A rule of thumb could be to ensure your child sees *you* valuing *yourself* in the same way you would like to see them valuing themselves.

Competitiveness

Sometimes, the management of, or lack of ability to manage mistakes, comes from a child's own feelings and behaviour in competitive situations. Levels of competitiveness vary between each child and is very much down to temperament and personality traits. Of course, home environments play a role, and highly competitive parents and households are often more likely to raise competitive children - although this is not definitive, and sometimes siblings brought up in the same environment, can differ greatly.

Competitiveness can be healthy - it helps us figure out what we want and what is important to us. This helps us learn more about who we are as a person, which can increase our own self-awareness; this being a key goal of Therapy and an important aspect of positive mental health. Being competitive can also push us to achieve goals and work harder, which at times can be beneficial to our self-esteem.

On the other hand, for someone who is overly competitive, this can lead to difficulties when feelings of self-worth become solely based around achievements. When we are too driven, or compare ourselves too much to others, it can also become self-destructive when our main goal is to succeed above those around us. This can impact meaningful relationships and be a cause of high levels of stress and anxiety. Like with most things discussed in this book, and in fact, like with most things in life - we need to strive to find a healthy balance.

Perhaps spend a few moments using the 'Notes' section of the book to reflect on your child's levels of competitiveness. Has it ever given you cause for concern? Maybe try to think back to some situations when your child was playing games or participating in matches or challenges, how did they react?

Briefly consider your own levels of competitiveness. It is not uncommon for family games to turn into serious rivalry and although this can be humorous, consider what message this is portraying, if you notice yourself becoming very competitive around your child. Is it demonstrating too much of an importance in winning? Monitor your own behaviour - are you playing to have fun, or are you playing to 'win' - how do you react when you lose? How do you react when you win? Do you accept gracefully, or do you wind others up? If you are over competitive, try to save this for games when it is just you and other adults, or for times at work, and where possible lower this when around your child.

Winning and losing

Play is a child's natural language, and in some types of play there will be levels of competitiveness when it involves having a clear 'winner' and 'loser'. How does your child cope? Can they manage loss? Do they always need to win? Do they consider they have failed if they do not win?

I have worked with numerous children in Therapy sessions who just cannot fathom the thought of losing any sort of game and will go to great lengths to ensure that this does not happen - even if that means insisting on changing the rules of play. This idea of not being able to lose is common for many children, especially pre-schoolers and 'cheating' in order to win can be a natural part of childhood development. However, as children mature and begin their primary school years, it is very important for them to learn that winning is not always possible and that losing is not 'failing'.

Wanting to win is a natural human instinct and early childhood is often about experiencing winning and losing and learning how to cope and manage this. When playing with our children it can be very tempting to steer clear of competitive situations or to 'let them win' to avoid the challenging tantrum or meltdown that may ensue should they lose. However, experiencing loss is a fundamental learning opportunity. For a child who is always allowed to win, even though this may give them immediate satisfaction, it is not necessarily conducive to overall positive mental health. If a child has spent their entire early years winning at everything they do, I am sure you can imagine what a travesty it may feel to them when suddenly they learn this is not always the case - for example, when they play in their first match at school and lose the tournament. However upset your child may be at the time, they are gaining fundamental skills in resilience and resilience equates to a huge aspect of positive mental health.

Of course, a child needs to experience the validation over success and winning too. If they are playing against you, an adult, they need to win sometimes too, but ensure this is within a balance.

Accepting loss and mistakes

Family board games are wonderful opportunities to interact together and as mentioned in the 'Expressing Feelings and Emotions' chapter they can provide wonderful opportunities for mental health development. In terms of this topic, they can be a powerful way of helping to build resilience, by supporting a child in experiencing both loss and success / validation. If you and your child rarely play board games, it could be worth investing in a few fun games and beginning some family traditions of game nights.

If you feel your child already struggles a little when it comes to winning and losing, initially consider some team games, like 'Charades'. This can primarily be helpful for a child to start to experience loss as a team, rather than an individual. Sometimes losing a game but knowing others in your team are in the same situation as you, can be a great starting point in accepting a loss.

Teaching by example, (remember so much of what primary aged children learn is observational) is one of the simplest ways to help children learn to control their reactions to losing in play. Allow your child to see you lose and see how you overcome the disappointment of not winning. Let them see you congratulate your opponents and demonstrate how you can be gracious. Support your child by not letting them see you internalise the loss, but instead point out aspects of your own performance that you were proud of in the game.

Explaining the notion of 'chance' to children can also be useful. Many children think they have the power to control the entire game (including the way the dice falls). It is not uncommon for a child to think if they hold the dice a certain way, or blow on it, or say a magic word, the dice will do as they wish! However, this feeling of power can feel stressful and from time to time knowing that certain aspects of play is out of their hands, can be helpful to cope with loss, and not internalise it as a failure. The older they get, help your child to learn that they cannot control everything around them, including the behaviours and actions of others. For example, they can accept the loss of a team match, by knowing *they* did their best, but cannot control how others played or how many goals others scored etc. This is important for those involved in team activities and sports, as it is natural for some children to blame the entire loss of a tournament on themselves, not taking into account that there were multiple other children in the match too. Always remember to praise your child's efforts whether the team lost or won.

All the pointers in our 'Expressing Feelings and Emotions' chapter are very important in relation to this topic, in helping your child verbalise how they may feel after losing - "can you tell me how you feel?" or "perhaps you are feeling annoyed your sister won". This helps them to accept that these feelings are natural and OK. This empathy can in time reduce tantrums that result due to losing in play. Remember some younger children are still developing this concept of winning and losing, so compassion towards their emotionally, overwhelming feelings is important.

Everyday mistakes

It is also important to briefly bear in mind that a primary school child's body and mind is continually developing, meaning at times they can behave inappropriately or act in ways that may appear careless. Sometimes this may be the case, if their mind is elsewhere, but other times it can be simply because your child is still learning. We as adults may instinctively know the correct way to hold something and exactly when to turn off the tap when the water jug is nearly full, or the right pressure to place on an object in order not to break it, but your child is still figuring this out. Try to consider your own attitudes towards your child when minor, everyday mistakes like this occur. Although children need to learn appropriate ways to carry out tasks, it is also important that they do not develop a fear of trying, or an internal belief that they are 'silly' or 'incapable'. If they worry about completing minor tasks, then this will translate into a much bigger worry, when it comes to engaging in more 'important' tasks.

Encouraging a growth mindset

A 'Fixed Mindset', for example, "I cannot do maths" can hold children back from learning and can affect their overall mental health when they view setbacks and difficulties as overwhelming. The notion of a 'Growth Mindset' was originally coined by Professor Carol Dweck and is something many schools now focus on, as a way of encouraging more positive learning. A growth mindset quite simply is a concept that relates to how we manage challenges and setbacks. It helps a child to accept that abilities and intelligence are not fixed and can be adapted and improved, over time, with perseverance and hard work.

Children who are supported in developing this growth mindset tend to encounter challenges in a more positive way, often showing increased self-esteem and resilience - two huge factors contributing to positive mental health.

Let us look at a few examples of what exactly we mean by these two different mindsets. The first phrase in each pairing demonstrates the thinking process of someone with a 'fixed mindset' and the bold phrase reveals the thinking process of someone with a **'growth mindset'**.

"I cannot do my homework. I do not understand maths"

"I cannot do this homework yet. I do not understand this maths equation"

"I am terrible at tennis"

"I need to practise my serves a little more"

"I am never going to understand this"

"I am not good at this yet, but if I practise more, and try a different strategy I can improve"

"I am never going to be good at this"

"I need to ask my teacher some questions tomorrow so I can figure this out"

"I can never build a sandcastle"

"I need to add more water, then it may work"

"I cannot play the piano at all"

"I cannot play this new piece yet, but I will be able to if I keep trying"

Slight re-framing of thought processes can aid the development of this positive mindset, changing our thinking from something that is fixed, final and permanent, to something that is malleable, and we *can* control.

Of course, it would be unrealistic to imagine children saying these growth mindset phrases out loud - after all, life is not scripted perfectly! However, a growth mindset, can encourage these *internal* thinking patterns within a child, helping them independently find solutions and cope with difficulties. A child who has developed a growth mindset, internally believes that over time their abilities can improve. A child who has not developed this will think their abilities are set in stone and naturally will be more inclined to give up at the first sign of difficulty. If we as adults believed something could never improve, no matter what we did, would we not want to give up too? If a child is convinced that they are *'terrible at tennis'* and no amount of hard work will change this, why would they want to persevere? This 'give up' attitude is understandable, but is also likely to link to mental health decline when their own self-belief is limited.

This idea can also be linked to interpersonal relationships, if a child has a fixed mindset about a peer or teacher, this may hold them back from developing crucial and fundamental relationships.

The good news is that there is lots that parents can do to support this more positive thinking style, thus supporting overall emotional health. As with everything discussed in this book, this is about a way of life, and not just trying ideas once or twice. Of course, if some of the forthcoming ideas differ to how you operate, then it will take time to develop new habits. There is no expectation that after reading this book you will suddenly begin to automatically follow all the suggested guidance. Over time, with patience and perseverance, slight amendments can be introduced at home, which with practise, eventually will feel natural and second nature.

All of the points at the start of this chapter, in relation to sharing your own mistakes with your child, being aware of how you verbalise out loud your own internal feelings and the ideas around playing games, winning, losing and competitiveness, are all helpful to consider in relation to encouraging a growth mindset. The following points add further ideas, in relation to building a positive mindset within your child, and thus supporting positive mental health.

1. Encouraging a growth mindset at home: Your own mindset

Consider your own mindset - have you ever caught yourself saying that you are terrible at cooking, singing or sports etc? Perhaps you have a belief that people are born a certain way and are naturally inclined to be 'good' or 'bad' at certain skills. Monitor your own beliefs and consider whether there could be notions of a 'fixed mindset' that you may be unintentionally passing on to your child.

2. Encouraging a growth mindset at home: Consider effort over achievements

Praising efforts and not just achievements is fundamental in helping primary aged children to grow up emotionally healthy. Many of the activities that we all engage in, have some form of end result. We can feel very disappointed if we do not meet that or meet our own expectations of what we felt we should have achieved. If there is too much focus on the outcome, children can learn that they only succeed if they reach this final goal, meaning everything along the way and the effort put into the task was irrelevant.

Getting into the habit of focusing on effort, not just achievements is so important - although this is easier said than done and it can take time to feel natural and heartfelt doing so. Reflect out loud how *hard* your child worked, the *care* they took when they created something, the *idea* behind the artwork and consider your use of words when congratulating them. Although saying "your painting is beautiful" is also important, re-phrasing this at times, to focus on the effort and path it took to get to the final result is powerful. For example, "I can see all the hard work you put in there using different brush strokes on that tree". This can be relevant to many areas in your child's life. Praise and comment on all the amazing running they did up and down the pitch for the whole match, rather than on how many goals were scored; how well they concentrated when following that recipe, rather than on how the cake tasted and how much effort they put in trying to remember their spellings, rather than the final mark.

When the attention is too much on the outcome, and this unfortunately goes wrong, some children can really struggle. In these situations, it is also important to monitor how you respond to your child's school results / assessments, ensuring that you focus on the effort and how hard they tried too.

Activities whereby you can focus on the process, not just the outcome, may include:

· Baking with your child.

· Going shopping for a gift for their friend - consider the thoughtful, kind, thinking processes necessary when deciding what the other person may like, not just talking about the gift itself.

· A DIY project together - the effort it takes to learn how to use the new tools, not just the final result.

· Learning a brand new skill together - both learning and making mistakes together on the way.

· Creating a vegetable garden together - focusing on the effort put in to tend and care for the plants.

It can also be useful to look into playing some fun games and activities which do not involve winning or losing. There are some entertaining games on the market which are not about keeping score, but just about being silly together. This can help a child see that enjoyment can be had, even if there are no final achievements.

Bear in mind your weekend activities too; can you find enjoyable things to do as a family, which do not involve any form of competitiveness.

3. Encouraging a growth mindset at home: What could be done differently?

When things do not always go to plan, monitor your own behaviour towards your child's mistakes. How do you react when they come home saying they failed their maths quiz, or lost their sports tournament? Although as parents we will all have our own different expectations of our children, dependent on our own family set-up, values, and beliefs, it is important to make sure your expectations are realistic and achievable for each of your children.

Rather than expressing your disappointment towards a result your child has shared, it can sometimes be helpful to gently and with empathy, sit with them and think of what they could do differently next time? What can they learn from this if they had to do it again? Do they need you, or their teacher to go over anything with them? This is not only teaching positive solution-finding skills, but supports children in learning that they have the power and ability to alter their performance next time. They can leave the conversation feeling more content that they have an idea and a plan for next time, rather than feeling low and hopeless.

4. Encouraging a growth mindset at home: The power of the brain

Teach your child about the plasticity of the brain (in age-appropriate terms!) and how we can 'grow' our brain, just like we can grow our muscles in our body to be strong. Educate them that practise, continued perseverance, and effort when things are tricky can grow our brain, just in the same way exercise can grow our muscles too. Explain how amazing it is that brains can actually get stronger and stronger, the more we do. Children often appreciate it when adults converse with them in this mature manner and feel respected and motivated.

Sometimes using metaphors or imagery for children can be useful in building a picture for them. Dependent on the age of your child you could, for example, help them to imagine our brains as having millions and billions of little light bulbs, each representing something different. A maths light bulb, a spellings light bulb, a tennis light bulb, a riding a bike light bulb, a flying a rocket light bulb etc. There are light bulbs for everything! Although of course sometimes these light bulbs never turn on at all, as we cannot do everything, and no one is great at everything.

When we participate in something, the light bulb turns on. For example, the first time we ride our bike, that light bulb glows a tiny little bit. The more we practise on our bike, the brighter that bulb gets. This is the same for our schoolwork; initially the bulbs are really low, or even off, because we are still learning, but practise helps them glow brighter and brighter each time. The brighter our bulbs are, the stronger our brain is getting.

This notion can help children understand that even if they initially cannot do something the first, or second, or third time, it is important to keep trying. This builds fundamental resilience, which down the line can support children in managing unexpected troubling times.

5. Encouraging a growth mindset at home: Remind them of previous successes

This can go alongside, or separate to the light bulb analogy, but supporting children in remembering their previous growth can help. For example, "when you started year two, you were doing four-letter spellings which you found tricky. Now look at you, you are learning eight-letter words" or "when you first got your scooter, balancing was a little difficult and you held my hand, but your practise paid off and you don't even need my help now!"

Initiating conversations like this with your child, helps to install memories of previous frustrations which were overcome.

6. Encouraging a growth mindset at home: Introduce the word 'yet'

Never underestimate the power of the three-letter word - YET! This word encompasses so much when it comes to supporting this positive style of thinking. Adding it to children's natural phrases when they complain to you about frustrations, helps them to also see your own faith and belief in them. The more you add this word to their dialogue, the more, in time, they will internally use this themselves.

"I cannot do this equation... (yet)"

"I cannot do my zip up... (yet)"

7. Encouraging a growth mindset at home: Famous failings

Something that can be really helpful for a child to be aware of, is knowing that their 'idols' also encountered struggles too. It is often easy for a child to see their favourite pop icon, sports figure, or YouTube star as someone who always succeeds, however knowing that 'famous people' also experience setbacks is important. If your child particularly likes a well-known media figure, spend some time researching that person and what they did prior to becoming so well known. There are many famous faces who spent years trying to achieve, encountering numerous obstacles, attending countless auditions, or starting various online channels with no success. Often young children are unaware of this. Educating your child in this manner can help them see that mistakes and things going wrong are a natural part of life for everyone and that it is the journey and effort that is so imperative. It can also help a child to accept and move on with a positive attitude from things they may have 'failed' at. This can also apply to *your* successes too – let your know child know how many attempts it took you to pass your driving test, or how many interviews you had before you got your 'dream job'.

Giving some consideration to, and possibly changing your own viewpoint on mistakes whilst taking into account the importance of how you respond when things do go wrong, is so important for our children's mental health. Just like adults, children have good days, bad days, and days when it may feel like everything is going wrong. In order to cope with the later demands of adolescence and adult life, children need to gain these resilience skills from an early age, helping them to cope, move on and bounce back from mistakes and difficult times.

Key 'takeaways' from this chapter to support positive mental health:

- ✓ Be aware how children can develop negative thought patterns, viewing themselves and their abilities only based on their achievements and successes

- ✓ Consider your own expectations of your child and your responses when things may go wrong for them, or they do not 'achieve' to your standards

- ✓ Be aware of how levels of competitiveness, the desire to win in play and general everyday mistakes can impact a child's developing sense of self

- ✓ Consider the differences between a 'fixed mindset' and a 'growth mindset' and ways to support the latter within your child

CHAPTER NINE

Self-care

Therapeutic Goals to be considered at home:

· Supporting children from a young age to develop positive self-care skills

· Helping children to understand associations between their needs and behaviours that they should or should not engage in

How this builds Positive Mental Health:

· Helps a child feel resilient and able to cope and care for themselves in everyday life and during times of stress

· Helps a child learn which behaviours may increase their stress and when to avoid these

Self-care can be defined as taking action to preserve or improve one's own health and protecting one's own well-being and happiness, in particular, during periods of stress. Not only is this fundamental for parents to practise (which we will briefly explore), but educating children on self-care, from a young age, can potentially reduce possible mental health conditions later in life.

Habits are easier to maintain than they are to create, therefore the earlier your child learns fundamental self-care skills, the more likely they are to continue these as they mature.

When thinking about our children, the following would be considered useful pointers in terms of self-care:

· Personal hygiene / basic care / cleanliness

· Diet / food intake

· Sleep / down time

· Responses to stress / mood changes

· Exercise

· Socialising / peer associations

· Interests / passions

It is important, as parents, to help our children identify the associations between the listed self-care pointers. For example, how does diet affect my sleep? How does sleep affect my mood? How does my friend affect how I feel? How does my mood change when I go running? This understanding of association is an invaluable skill to support positive mental health throughout the primary school years and beyond.

By following the previous guidance in this book, you are in fact already working on your child's self-care, through encouraging them to express their emotions and feelings, monitoring routines and schedules, ensuring appropriate amounts of stress-free down time, establishing suitable sleep patterns, supporting healthy friendships and helping them identify bodily sensations which may be triggers for worry or anxiety. All of these topics help to support a child's emotional health and are setting them up with the right 'tools' for a positive and healthy future lifestyle.

There are however a few more ideas that we will consider within this chapter in relation to your child's self-care.

Many of the young people I work with in secondary school often lack this understanding around their own self-care and although positive changes can still be made, it is often more difficult starting these new habits in the teenage years, when children are not so adaptable.

One of the main goals in relation to self-care in children, is encouraging your child to learn to recognise their own needs and what appropriate steps they can take to meet these. During primary school, children may not always independently be able to fulfil these requirements alone, but gaining an understanding of them, and developing positive habits will stand them in good stead for when they are older and less dependent on you. Although this book focuses on primary school children, the following case study demonstrates how easy it is for teenagers to develop negative patterns and mental health difficulties, when an understanding around self-care is lacking.

Case Study: Simaya aged 14

Simaya had experienced a very stable childhood, with little change and her parents never had any concerns about her mental health until she entered secondary school. She initially came to Therapy struggling with excessive stress (mainly down to the school workload) which was beginning to cause her to have mild panic attacks. Simaya's parents were also concerned about her becoming depressed, noticing she had let her personal hygiene slip, and no longer seemed to enjoy activities that she used to. It is important to note that lack of self-care and a lack of interest in previous hobbies can be signs of potential depression, but fortunately this was not the case for Simaya. Quite simply, she had got herself into a negative stress-response behavioural pattern, which was then spiralling a little out of control. Simaya had no idea how to make herself feel better when worried or stressed and to combat this she began eating excessive amounts of chocolate every day. The sugar rush would initially make her feel better, so she assumed it was helping. This excessive snacking after school caused Simaya's appetite to change. She would not need so much food in the evening, meaning valuable nutrients from 'healthy meals' were being missed. Simaya's weight did not fluctuate, so her parents assumed she was still eating well at school and was simply not as hungry later in the day. This long-term change in diet affected her sleep, which eventually impacted Simaya's moods. She had little energy to exercise or socialise and her personal hygiene was no longer a priority to her. Showers took too much energy. Poor personal hygiene, poor diet and a lack of exercise meant that Simaya began having trouble with her skin. This led her to avoid parties, due to her self-esteem and confidence decreasing, which then spiralled into conflict with friends, who were angry she did not spend time with them. Quite simply, everything felt out of control for Simaya, with one decision affecting another, thus having an impact on her overall mental health and well-being.

Simaya did not need long-term support in terms of Therapy. A large part of our work was helping her develop connections between her behaviours and the consequences of them. Through this, we were able to discuss imperative self-care skills and start associating how certain actions made changes to her mood. For example, how did she feel after a walk / fresh air / a shower / a face mask / seeing friends / a fresh meal or too much chocolate? These associations can be tricky to make independently, but were exactly what Simaya needed to help her see that there was nothing 'wrong' with her, she just needed some lifestyle changes.

Negative behavioural patterns can develop easily, and I am sure, even as adults, you may be able to recall some days, or weeks that lifestyle factors may have soared out of control, influencing your overall mood and health. For a teenager, this is common, especially when so much change is occurring around them. We can, however, strive to reduce the chance of this happening by educating and equipping young children with these skills, and the understanding of associations and self-care.

How to support self-care skills at home

Your own verbalisation to your child can considerably develop this understanding and awareness around their specific needs and what can be done to support these. For example, if they are feeling extremely tired after a late night, vocalise ideas they could try... "Tonight you need to have an early night to catch up on sleep" / "Perhaps you need to relax on the sofa for an hour" / "Maybe having a warm, relaxing bath might make you feel better and be just what you need" / "This would be a good breakfast to have, to give you the energy you need before school".

The aforementioned phrases are instinctive knowledge that we take for granted as an adult, but if we do not clearly explain these to our children, how are they meant to know that they have the power to help themselves, when they are not feeling quite on top of things? If we just put our child to bed 30-minutes earlier, or prepare an energy-inducing meal for them, without letting them know in what way these strategies can benefit them, how will they ever learn?

When our child is starting to feel a little unwell, we may give them medicine, add in a daily vitamin supplement / an extra piece of fruit in their lunch box, or encourage them to spend some time in the sunshine to boost their natural vitamin D. All instinctive parental behaviours, with often no explanation to our child. Imagine how valuable and beneficial it could be, to express in words your actions, in order to support their overall independent health as they get older. For Simaya, she simply had no idea how to make herself feel better in times of difficulty. If we do everything for our children, without adding in some education too, it is likely they will not independently feel empowered to help themselves.

This very much applies to times of stress or worry too. It is important to help our children understand what they 'need' to support them when they are feeling a little low. As we have mentioned before, your child will watch how you cope and what works for you. Do you go to the gym or go on a run when you have had a stressful day? Do you listen to music? What are your stress-busting mechanisms? Of course, what works for you may not work for your child, and it is about figuring this out together. Supporting your child in learning to identify a feeling of stress, and then learning what they can do to improve their mood is fundamental for positive mental health. This can empower children and build their confidence and self-esteem knowing that they have the 'power', at times, to make themselves feel better.

Figuring out what helps your child after a tough or stressful day is trial and error. Maybe painting will make one child feel better, but meditation may help another. Maybe one child likes to have a good run around, whereas another needs to relax and colour. Experiment together, then when something seems to work, support your child in using this idea on another occasion when they appear stressed. They will, in time, learn independently what is right for them; for example, a slightly older child / young teenager, may realise they need to go for a walk to 'clear their head'.

It can be beneficial to teach children the science behind some of these ideas - exercise releases 'endorphins' which can make us feel happy; fresh air helps our body produce vitamins, which can make us feel energised. Too much sugar can make us feel great in the moment, but tired later. The more factual information we give our child, the more likely they are to listen and take heed.

This also works in the opposite way too - help your child learn the things that do *not* make them feel good. For example, a late night watching films or staying up for a sleepover may be fun at the time, but how do they feel the next day? What has happened to their mood? Do they still have the energy to do fun things? Eating a giant bar of chocolate may have been tasty there and then, but how do they feel 2-hours later? These associations are not always instinctive, and your child needs you, as their first educator, to support them in learning these behaviour-to-feeling links. Try your best not to criticise the behaviour and refrain from expressing an 'I told you so' attitude. Naturally, this can be hard, especially if you are annoyed that your child did not go to sleep when asked and they are now moody and listless. Remember though, if a child does not get the chance to encounter these associations first-hand, they will never learn that certain behaviours are likely to cause particular feeling responses. We cannot expect them to just take our word for it - they need to experience them, in order to then use that knowledge and apply it to other self-care related situations.

Personal hygiene and basic care

This may seem unrelatable to mental health, but many teenagers will naturally let showering and washing their hair slip, when things around them are stressful. The effects of poor hygiene and lack of personal care in this way can cause low moods, diminished self-esteem, poor body image, avoidance of social situations and little motivation; all of which have the power to spiral out of control and cause mental health decline. It is for this reason it is imperative to educate children on the importance of maintaining their own personal hygiene and care independently. For much younger children, it is natural for parents to want to do these things for them, especially in modern-day busy households when time is in short supply. However, by modelling patience and perseverance, it is far more beneficial for your child's self-belief, confidence and self-care understanding, if they can explore how to do things for themselves - even if this is initially frustrating and time consuming for you.

It is not uncommon for children of around eight years old to enter early puberty, and personal hygiene is also of particular importance during these years, for example, with regards to changing body odours. Body changes and self-consciousness, even in the primary years can impact a child's confidence, which can impact their mental health. Setting your child up with these basic, but imperative skills, from the start of primary school may seem minor, but can make a huge impact on overall health. Respecting personal hygiene and care, also helps children to develop a further understanding of the importance of good health which is important as they grow and develop.

Your own self-care

We have probably all heard the safety announcement on an aeroplane about putting on your own oxygen mask, before helping others, and quite simply, this is because no one can support and care for those around them, if they are not in good health themselves. This applies to everyday parenting too. You cannot support your child's mental health, if yours is suffering, therefore taking time for yourself and your own needs is not selfish - it is imperative.

Self-care is important in order for you to maintain a positive relationship with yourself, which can help boost your own self-esteem and confidence. Consider your own needs and interests, away from your child and make time for these. As we have frequently mentioned, so much of what children learn is observational, therefore the more a child sees mum / dad taking care of themselves and respecting their bodies, the more likely it is a child will follow their example.

Key 'takeaways' from this chapter to support positive mental health:

- ✓ Children are never too young to learn basic self-care skills
- ✓ Consider verbalising to your child the things you instinctively do to support their health, helping them develop associations between their own needs and activities they can choose to engage in
- ✓ Assess with your child what does and does not help them during times of stress
- ✓ Encourage your child's independent skills and awareness around basic care and personal hygiene
- ✓ Consider your own needs and self-care requirements as parents

CHAPTER TEN

Factors Beyond Your Control

Therapeutic Goals to be considered at home:

· To build children's resilience and confidence in order to manage and cope with stressors outside of their home life

How this builds Positive Mental Health:

· Helps a child feel able to positively respond to unavoidable stress, without other areas of their life becoming too impacted

Most of this book focuses on empowering parents and discusses situations that you can strive to control *at home*, in order to support your child's mental health. However, what about certain situations that are beyond your control; the experiences and situations outside of the home environment that you cannot necessarily predict, or prevent?

Loss and grief, marital breakdowns, traumas, relocations, family conflict and more, are a few life events that some children will have to encounter and manage in their life. Many of the chapters in this book are about building and maintaining your child's overall mental health, long-term, in order to encourage and support them in being able to cope the best they can, should unfortunate situations arise.

The following chapter will now briefly explore two common, important topics, that almost *all* children in primary school will encounter at some point and that will be, to an extent, beyond your control. Nevertheless, you can equip yourselves with 'tools' that will help you to manage the repercussions of these events.

'Worldly events' and 'friendships' - two completely contrasting subjects, but two topics that are a factor of everyday life, even for children. Almost no child will go through primary school without encountering some form of difficulty in relation to peers. It is also true that sadly all children will inevitably hear about, at some point, an awful event that has happened somewhere in the world, maybe even in their own country, or local town.

Both these subjects can cause stress, worry, anxiety and behavioural changes, all affecting a child's mental health. You may not be able to prevent the initial worry, or stop the actual event or scenario happening, but you can help your child deal with what has occurred, appropriately, ensuring their mental health does not decline long-term as a result.

If supported in the right way, sometimes these events beyond our control have the power to strengthen mental health, helping children to feel strong and resilient and able to cope when future stressors and difficulties arise.

1. **Worldly Events**

Unfortunately, there are always going to be terrible situations happening in the world that your child may hear about. Natural disasters, wars, terrorist attacks, large spread illnesses, and more, are sadly common occurrences. If you think back to the last few years, I am sure you can recall multiple events of this kind that have featured heavily in the news.

Hopefully, many of these situations will not be close to home and the majority will not personally impact your child at all. Often, however, just hearing about these through the media, or from those around them, can still evoke intense feelings of anxiety and stress in some children.

After the London Bridge and Westminster terrorist attacks in London, many of my subsequent Therapy sessions, (despite no children I worked with being directly impacted at all) focused around anxieties that had stemmed from what they had heard, pictures they had seen and 'what if' thoughts. What if it happened again? What if it happened where I was? What if my parents were in the proximity? These children had an outlet for their concerns in their Therapy sessions, and fortunately after a couple of weeks their worries generally subsided.

For children who do not have, or do not need a Therapist, their outlet for this needs to be their parents. Anxiety and intrusive thoughts can develop into obsessive thinking and worrying, when a child is unable to seek reassurance or share their concerns with an appropriate adult.

It is natural to want to shield children from these events and you may even be thinking now that there is no reason for your child to even be told about them. It is important to remember nonetheless, that school aged children are away from you for often over 6-hours a day, meaning you are not in full control of what they are hearing or discussing.

During the Grenfell Tower fire in West London in 2017, it was interesting how in the days and weeks that followed, many of the children I worked with would play out games involving fire, people being trapped and death. These children were in early primary school and lived nowhere near the incident and knew no one involved. On checking in with their parents, most mums / dads told me that they had no idea their child was even aware about the Grenfell fire.

During the Covid-19 Pandemic of 2020, even before the Government initiated a UK lockdown, I saw very young children of four or five years engaging in play involving 'masks' and 'protection' with themes often based around poison, getting ill or medical emergencies. Play of this kind is usually nothing to be concerned about and in fact, can be healthy - it is a child's way of processing what they feel is going on around them. It does demonstrate though, how much children, including the very young, become aware of events, even if these have not been shared directly with them by their family. Perhaps Hannah in your child's class was told by her mum last night what happened, and Hannah is now in school sharing facts with her peers. The problem here, is that in peer environments, facts get distorted and inappropriate, or inaccurate knowledge may be communicated, which can add to the worry and confusion for a child.

Remember to also consider that children may hear information when the news is on the TV or radio in your home or car - children absorb everything they hear. This chapter is not suggesting that every child should be shielded from the news, but if it is on, make sure you are with them, so you can explain or answer any questions they may have. Try and see your role as parents as the 'filter' - it is your job to take in what has happened, understand it, and *filter* it back to your child in a way that they can understand.

The following pointers are useful to have in your 'toolbox' should a highly unfortunate event in the world occur. They can also be helpful for closer to home matters, such as local burglaries and / or general crimes where you live.

Although these techniques are useful for many different topics, for the sake of clarity we shall just name the worldly event as 'the situation' in the bullet points listed.

· Try to ask your child what they already know about the situation. This gives you an opportunity to learn more about their knowledge and if it is inaccurate or extorted beyond the truth.

· Consider the vocabulary that your child may be hearing, such as 'terrorist', 'earthquake' or 'bomb'. These are words young children are unlikely to have in their general vocabulary. Hearing words that they do not understand can be scary. Help to explain, in age-appropriate terms, the words they are hearing, in order to lessen the fear. Often the 'unknown' is responsible for many anxieties developing, as everything becomes magnified in a child's mind.

· Ask your child if they have any questions about the situation, listen clearly, but do not push if there is nothing they wish to ask.

· If you do not know the answer, tell your child that you will try and find out and return to them later with a response. Make sure you follow this up, so they know you have remembered their concern. Being honest with a child and telling them you are unsure right now, is far better than making something up. Most children can tell when someone close to them is not being honest and it is important that your child develops a complete belief in what you are saying - otherwise it is possible they will not trust you when you reassure them.

· Listen to your child's worries and fears and give them opportunities and space to talk and share, whilst reassuring them where possible. Of course, in many situations, for example, if there has been a terrorist attack, you cannot guarantee that this will never happen again. However, you can offer confident reassurance of how unlikely it is to affect them directly. Validate their feelings, so they know it is completely natural to feel uneasy right now. We do not want children worrying, on top of the situation, that how they are feeling is not OK.

· Talk with your child about all the adults in their life who care and look after them and explain to them how these individuals are here to protect them. This can also include teachers, as well as emergency workers like the police, fire officers and medical staff. In some situations, where appropriate, you could even go into more detail, explaining how there are certain helpers in the world who practise dealing with situations like this, so they have plans in place if they do occur. Children need to feel secure with the adults around them.

· Dependent on what the situation is, your child may need clearly reminding of all the things at home that protect them (for example, locks and alarm systems etc.) and all the things at home that you do as a family that keep them well, healthy and safe from harm.

· Try to remain as calm as possible when talking to your child. Monitor your tone of voice and come down to their level so you can offer touch as a comfort too. If you seem panicked, your child will pick up on this.

· Be aware of speaking about the situation to others when your child is in the room, or in close proximity. It is so important to remember, even when engaged in something else, children still have ears and can hear! Keep adult conversations about the situation, even with your partner, for times when your child is in bed, or out the house.

· Perhaps consider speaking with the parents of your child's close friendship group so you can all be on the same page about what is being shared.

· Speak with your child's teacher, so you are aware of how the school is dealing with the situation and what is being explained to the different age groups.

· For older children who have their own phone, you may need to monitor their usage a little more, to ensure that they are not seeing or reading anything inappropriate, adding extra worry.

· For younger children, monitor their play to see if internal anxieties may be coming out. There is more on this in the next chapter 'General Worries and Anxieties', but it is common after a big event for children's play to involve themes around danger and rescue scenes.

· Consider watching with your child certain beneficial programmes, like the news on children's television channels. These are designed to educate in an age-appropriate way, whilst not creating panic. Watching it with them allows you to offer reassurance, clarity and answer any questions.

· Children often worry about their family members, just as much as themselves. It may offer them extra comfort to video call their grandparents, or distant relatives and friends more often that week. This is not to discuss the situation, but just as a reassurance that those they love are safe and well and life is continuing as 'normal'.

· Continue to check-in with your child and make sure they are coping and able to express any thoughts.

· Try your best to keep all routines at home exactly the same. This will provide stability and consistency, helping to alleviate stress and anxiety.

· Try to have fun with your child, to refocus their mind and let them see all the good there still is in the world.

It is natural for children's behaviour to temporarily change when there are high levels of stress or worry around them and it is likely this would be more apparent if 'the situation' was close to home, or directly involved your child. It can also be common for children in primary school to 'regress' to a younger style of behaviour, such as bed wetting or having excessive tantrums, as their way of striving to cope with events. Although these behaviours can be challenging for parents, try to remind yourself that they are temporary and should lessen in time. Hopefully, the prior points regarding how you can support your child, will also help to alleviate some of these behaviours. Children may need extra comfort, hugs, love, attention, and increased patience during these times, which all are likely to take up more of your energy. If *you* are stressed and anxious, your child will pick up on this, so ensure you are also receiving extra support from those around you and supporting one another if you are a two-parent family. Children will benefit, the more emotionally healthy *you* feel.

2. **Friendships**

In contrast to the previous topic, let us take a few moments to examine another theme which is often completely beyond the control of parents - *the behaviour of your child's peers.*

For a child who attends school, friends are a fundamental aspect of their school journey. When I talk to a child in a Therapy session about school, the most common subject, and often something which appears most important to them, are the peers around them. Children are at school to learn, but what they are learning from a social viewpoint, is just as important as the academic side. A positive peer network is fundamental to mental health. It creates a feeling of security and helps a child develop positive self-esteem, feeling good about themselves, in the knowledge that others want to spend time with them. Friendships can help alleviate feelings of stress, whilst teaching children vital life skills and coping mechanisms, in terms of managing expectations, the needs of others and conflict.

It is not uncommon in the primary school years for children's friendships to shift and adapt and there are bound to be some difficulties along the way. Most of the time, children can manage these with the help of their parents, although at times friendship differences can cause a great deal of stress and upset. From my observation, I have found girls in year 4 or 5 tend to experience quite a lot of disruption, as well as children who are in a friendship group of three - although of course the latter is not definitive and many children manage well in these dynamics.

As children progress through primary school, they mature and enter puberty at different rates, meaning even the most stable of friendships can be impacted. At times, this can be very hard for parents to manage and it can feel heart breaking when your child comes home upset, over the way they may have been treated by another child.

Like worldly events, these peer difficulties also have the potential to strengthen mental health. Children learn ways to cope, and ways to respond to conflict as they mature, giving them the experience and confidence to bounce back from challenging times in the future.

Nonetheless, long-term friendship problems, without any support, can cause mental health decline. They can affect a child's self-esteem and feelings of worth and can also be the cause of children avoiding school, which can in turn develop into patterns of avoidance over any situation which triggers anxiety. This avoidance pattern can be difficult to break, therefore the sooner issues are dealt with, the better.

Here are some further points to consider when it comes to friendships during the primary school years.

Making friends

For some children, this does not come naturally and they may need a few pointers from *you.* This may also apply when your child starts a new club or activity away from school. It is easy and common to say to a child "go and make friends!" or "did you make any new friends today?" but have we ever actually taught them how? Here are a few tips that may be helpful.

· Support them with how to initiate an interaction. For example, if in a park or at a soft play centre and your child is hesitant to go off and join others, give them a little guidance.

For example: *"If you see someone you want to play with, you could go up to them, say hello, tell them your name and then ask them theirs".*

Often this starting point is just the help reticent children may require. Children may also need help with developing patience and understanding that not all connections are instant, and it can take time for trust and mutual enjoyment to develop.

· Teach children about their own body language and what others see when they look at them. If they are sitting, looking a little grumpy with their arms folded, what impression are they giving? If they are smiling and seeming friendly, that may make another child keen to play. Teach them how smiling at another child, can go a long way. Ask them how they feel when someone smiles at them? Then encourage them to do the same. You could act this out with your child, with you sitting in various positions, pulling different faces, so they can see how someone's body language and facial expression can be so influential. Ask them if they feel more inclined to play with you when you frown at them, or when you smile at them?

· Think of questions or 'conversation starters' that your child can have in their 'toolbox' to initiate a rapport with a new peer.

· Role-play this at home - you could be a new peer and your child can practise these conversation starters on you. With younger children, role-play using toys, or teddies.

· Suggest to your child that they could think of something kind to say to a new peer as an initiation - perhaps they like the child's bag, or hairstyle and they could share this thought with them. Ask your child how they feel when someone compliments them and suggest they could give this feeling to someone else too. Ideally, we would like children to learn to focus on and compliment others beyond just their appearance, or material possessions, but this can initially be hard for young children.

· When out in public, mirror to your child how you connect with others. Even if you do not really have the energy to be initiating a conversation with another parent in the local park, enabling your child *see* you do this, can give them the guidance and confidence to do the same.

Increasing networks and encouraging friendships

Some children may have 'one special best friend' and although this is incredibly positive, it is also important to consider (whilst still supporting that friendship) encouraging a wider network for your child. Unfortunately, I have worked with several primary school children, whose emotional health went into decline when their *one true best friend* moved away or changed schools and they simply could not cope without that person.

Although in-school peer relationships are fundamental, having one or two close friends who do not attend the same school can be supportive for children, widening their network. Attending clubs and extra-curricular activities can support this. This can be beneficial for your child offering them the security of knowing they have friends out of school too. In-school conflict tends to be more common, seeing as children spend considerable amounts of time in the same environment together, so external friends can be a welcome distraction.

Managing upsetting times

Unfortunately, parents are not in control of who their child will meet at primary school, and as discussed in our 'Expressing Feelings and Emotions' chapter, inevitably your child will meet peers who may treat them unkindly. The points on 'empathy towards others' in that chapter are very important when it comes to friendship difficulties, as this can help children remain self-assured and realise others' behaviours are due to their own personal circumstances, and not a personal attack on them. If you can, try and remain calm and level-headed, even if you do not feel it inside - your calmness will be contagious and will help your child. Validate your child's feelings, help them to understand why they are feeling this way, provide opportunities for 'talking time' and ensure not to belittle any of their minor concerns; these are all skills covered in previous chapters.

One of the biggest impacts of long-term friendship difficulties can be lowered self-esteem and self-worth. If your child has had a tough day, in terms of feeling left out by peers, they may need a little extra one-to-one time that evening, demonstrating to them how much you enjoy their company.

Healthy versus unhealthy friendships

Often with older primary school children, there will be times that they will need support in seeing 'through' particular friendships that are not necessarily 'healthy'. This can be so hard, as it is often these types of friendships that are challenging to let go of. Using these terms, 'healthy and unhealthy' with your child, can be helpful. Encourage your child to identify how certain peers make them feel, in comparison to other friendships which may feel 'happy' and 'easy.' This can be an important understanding to have before moving onto secondary school, when inevitably peer networks increase and can become more complex.

Sharing your own memories

Sharing your own memories of your peer experiences is important. If you can, try and name the other children in your stories, or even share photos of when you were at school, so that it feels even more real for your child. It will help them understand how even mum / dad had problems like theirs and they are not alone. Older siblings and cousins may also be helpful for your child to speak with.

Finding solutions together

With peer difficulties, it is often an immediate reaction to want to run into your child's school and speak to the teacher. Talk to your child first - find out what they *want* or *need* before you do anything. Sometimes simply just asking your child *"what do you need from me?"* can go a long way. In some scenarios, escalating it to the school, may not help your child - although of course, in situations involving bullying, this may be necessary. Thinking of solutions together with your child can be far more conducive to positive mental health and building resilience. This will also give them the skills to cope should this happen in the future.

If your child struggles to think of ideas, perhaps ask what 'advice' they would give a good friend or sibling if they happened to be in this situation. Sometimes it is easier for a child to take themselves out of the picture if they are directly involved.

You may need to work with the other parent on this, but sometimes encouraging children who are experiencing minor conflict to work together on a common goal, can be helpful. Perhaps they could plan a cake sale or organise a collection for charity. This takes the focus off the conflict and brings about feelings of altruism - which makes most people feel good!

Be aware of your child's role in the conflict

It is natural as parents to see the good in your child, but remember it is likely that there may be occasions that your child is partially at fault, and the conflict is not all down to the other peer. Your child may not have the self-awareness skills to reflect on their own behaviour, so you may need to gently help them do this. Ask them how they would feel, if they were being treated in the way they were treating their friend? If done in a supporting manner, this can be useful long-term, for your child's self-awareness development - a fundamental aspect of overall mental health. This can also stop similar situations escalating again in future.

Being aware of how your child sees *you* treating others is also important - remember so much of what children learn is observational.

Manage your child's expectations

When your child is sharing with you factors that may have happened with their peers, try to identify their 'expectations'. This may offer insight as to why they are feeling a certain way. Often children have unrealistic expectations of others (remember our case study of Darcie back in our 'Healthy Boundaries' chapter) and this can make friendships very troubling. They may 'expect' their 'best friend' to never play with anyone else but them, and this is unrealistic. Helping children in a gentle and kind way to have more acceptable and appropriate expectations of others, can help reduce conflict.

Sibling conflict translating into peer conflict

For some siblings who fight frequently, it can be natural to carry out these 'home behaviours' at school too. Your child may need your support in learning that some behaviours with their siblings are certainly not appropriate out of the home with their peers.

Encouraging respect between siblings can help with peer friendships too - although this may be asking the impossible for some, and sibling rivalry and conflict is natural!

Offer an outlet for emotions

Often when children are very upset by peer difficulties, this may come out in anger and frustration, causing them to lash out, or be unkind to others in retaliation. This can result in further problems and lack of resolution. It can sometimes be helpful to offer your child, at home, an outlet for these emotions and encourage them to *'let out their mad, without being mean'.*

If your child is feeling a strong dislike towards someone from school, resulting in displays of anger, think of ways to help them release their pent-up emotions. Kicking a ball outside really hard, going on a run together, punching their pillow (better to learn this safely now, then to feel the need to punch inappropriate things down the line, like people or walls), jumping and stamping on bubble wrap, ripping up newspaper, writing down feelings then ripping up the paper and squeezing playdough or putty could all be useful. This can help peer difficulties from escalating and turning physical.

Factors like 'Worldly Events' and 'Friendships' which are beyond your control as parents can be very tricky to manage and upsetting. Equipping yourself with the 'tools' to help your child manage such issues is important. Our next chapter 'General Worries and Anxieties' will offer more ideas for when children are impacted by different situations and events.

Remember though, it is difficult situations, like these, which can in fact, greatly build a child's resilience and positively impact on their future and mental health.

Key 'takeaways' from this chapter to support positive mental health:

- ✓ Equip yourself with skills to support your child should they encounter difficulties outside of the home and beyond your control
- ✓ Consider the key pointers in supporting your child's emotional well-being when concerning or upsetting worldly events occur
- ✓ Consider the key pointers to increase your confidence in supporting your child through friendship difficulties

CHAPTER ELEVEN

General Worries and Anxieties

In this penultimate chapter of the book, it is time to bring everything together that has been touched on and discussed throughout. Everything we have thought about so far, can all be considered in relation to one key factor of mental health... **anxiety.**

This is by far the most common reason why parents contact me for support for their child. Anxiety can manifest itself in so many different behaviours and can stem from a multitude of reasons. Sometimes it is clear why a child is anxious, particularly when it follows a specific experience or trauma; other times it is not so apparent. For some parents, it can feel like their child became anxious overnight, although usually this is unlikely, and it has probably been a build-up of triggers and stress, over time, that has caused this rapid change.

Anxiety can cause some children to become withdrawn and others to become overactive and aggressive. There is no one 'quick fix' to help any child who is overly anxious, given that each child responds differently. This chapter will discuss this in more detail, including ways to support your child and techniques to lower anxiety. Most importantly we will also recap on ways in which to *prevent* this escalation.

It is essential to remember that positive mental health is not just characterised by a lack of anxiety - there are so many fundamental aspects of life that help a child develop emotional health and resilience, which we have explored in our previous chapters.

However, pointers from all the previous chapters, can *also* be viewed as a way of *preventing anxiety from escalating*. Even without reading the new information in this chapter, everything you have absorbed in the book up to now, is all helpful in reducing anxiety in children, long-term. Let us remind ourselves of how...

Chapter 2 - **Expressing Feelings and Emotions**

We explored how we can prevent escalating anxiety by supporting a child's understanding of their body and their feelings.

Chapter 3 - **Encouraging Open Communication**

We explored how we can prevent worries and thoughts from being 'bottled up' internally, causing a build-up, down the line, of stress and anxiety.

Chapter 4 - **Schedules, Clubs and Free-Time**

We explored how we can ensure appropriate amounts of personal time are in place, to process inner thoughts through unstructured play and provide opportunities for relaxation and recharging the body - all preventing anxiety build-up.

Chapter 5 - **Developing Positive Sleep Patterns**

We explored how ensuring adequate levels of sleep each night, can encourage good attitudes, rational thoughts, and the development of positive thinking patterns; all of which can prevent increased anxiety.

Chapter 6 - **Technological Usage**

We explored how appropriate usage and safety online can prevent anxiety developing in children.

Chapter 7 - **Healthy Boundaries**

We explored how, by ensuring limits and boundaries are in place, we can prevent anxiety from building due to conflict, stress, and a lack of understanding around expectations.

Chapter 8 - **Making Mistakes, Failures and Coping When Things Go Wrong**

We explored ways to support our children when things do not go to plan, increasing their resilience skills and preventing anxiety from building due to a lowered self-belief.

Chapter 9 - **Self-care**

We explored ways children can learn invaluable self-care skills, to support their body and mind and strive to counteract stress, reducing anxiety.

Chapter 10 - **Factors Beyond our Control**

We explored ways of reducing stress and anxiety caused by external factors outside of the home.

I am not saying that all children who are overly anxious, are so because the previous ideas are not being followed. That is not the case at all, and often when I work with a child who is highly anxious, it is due to factors beyond their parents control - experiences and traumas that have inevitably had a great effect on them. Nonetheless, this book is about empowering parents with ways in which you can positively control the home environment, equip your child in primary school with knowledge, understanding and techniques to cope with anxiety, *before* it has built to a point that leads to unsafe behaviours.

Before we continue, it is important first to have some clarity on what exactly anxiety is and what levels we should consider to be 'appropriate' for a child.

'Worry' and 'anxiety' are often words used to describe a negative feeling, or a fear response and are frequently used inter-changeably. In fact, worry and anxiety differ greatly from one another, although distinguishing between the two can sometimes feel confusing, even for adults, let alone for a child.

In brief, although there are multiple explanations of the differences, one way we can compare them, is by considering that 'worry' is something we often feel in our head, whereas 'anxiety' is something we tend to feel more viscerally, in our body. For example, we might worry 'I am going to miss my bus', but feel the anxiety in our body as a strongly beating heart or accelerated breathing.

Worry also generally tends to be more realistic. For example, you are concerned you are going to lose your job because you are always late - whereas, anxiety is sometimes less rational. For example, you are concerned you are going to lose your job because your boss did not ask you about your child's school play.

Worry often triggers an anxiety response, and although we often think of 'anxiety' as negative, the right amount, at the right time, can in fact keep us safe and healthy. You may have heard that we need anxiety to keep us alive - it is in fact our body's natural response to stress or threat. Let us imagine the famous anxiety analogy of being in a forest and bumping into a bear - our immediate worry in our head is that 'he is going to eat me' - that worry alone is not going to save our life, but the anxiety that ensues, may. Our brain senses dangers and sends a series of signals to our bodies, activating the 'fight' or 'flight' response. For example, our heart beats extra fast, sending blood pumping around our bodies and to our legs, ready for a quick escape from the bear.

Therefore, anxiety in itself, is not a bad thing - not only can it help us when there is a potential threat, but it can also sometimes motivate us to work harder, for example, to complete a task that we are doubting we can do. If we are anxious about a forthcoming test, revising and working hard may alleviate some of that anxiety, resulting in a successful outcome.

It is natural and common for *everyone* to experience a certain amount of anxiety; it is part of life and not something to be concerned about. We all experience worry and anxiety, for example, in relation to our family, our finances and our health.

However, of course sometimes anxiety goes beyond what is 'acceptable'. Anxiety that is persistent, causing extreme avoidance of anxiety-provoking situations, resulting in impaired daily functions over a significant period of time, can possibly be seen as a *diagnosable anxiety disorder.*

Let us go back for a minute to your boss who did not ask about your child's school play. We can all have irrational fleeting thoughts like this, dependent on our mood and levels of tiredness. However, if this thought begins to take over everything, to the extent that you cannot talk to your boss, cannot go into the office for days, struggle to eat and sleep, then this may be seen as debilitating. It is going beyond natural levels of concern.

Sometimes teenagers I work with genuinely think they have a diagnosable anxiety disorder, when more often than not their anxiety is not actually debilitating or classified as a disorder - they are just in need of some 'tools' and support to manage it.

One thing I think is imperative for all children to learn throughout primary school is that general worry and anxiety is OK. I have found for some children, the thought of worrying and the physical sensations of anxiety can actually lead to further anxiety - because they are literally worrying about being worried. A child needs to know that it is natural to sometimes feel this way and that they can learn coping mechanisms in order to avoid issues escalating.

It is useful to help your child understand that sometimes a 'worry' may cause them to feel 'anxious'. Children need to know the common bodily symptoms of what happens when a worry causes anxiety. When they feel the anxious part coming on, they may need some help from mum / dad, or a teacher - and that is OK too. It can be worded in a very simple and age-appropriate way to help children understand.

An emotionally healthy child, in time, will be able to differentiate between a small worry and an anxious feeling. They will understand what is happening and usually be able to cope. This is fundamental for overall mental health, but of course it can take time to fully understand this.

Educating your child about anxiety

Before a child can begin to develop coping strategies, they first need to learn about anxiety - no one can learn how to cope with something, if they do not understand what they are trying to cope with in the first place. This would be like asking someone to grow and nourish an invisible plant, of which its requirements they know nothing about. How would they start?

The 'Expressing Feelings and Emotions' chapter discusses ways you can support your child in sharing and understanding their feelings, by verbalising your own feelings and emotions first. This is the same for worry and anxiety. Children need to see that *you* too have worries and anxiety. Naturally, limit what you share with your child - they do not need to know serious family matters causing you great stress, but you can discuss your own worries and anxiety in appropriate ways.

Perhaps your child has convinced you to go down a really steep slide at a soft play centre - you can share with them that you feel a little anxious and explain the bodily feelings that you may be experiencing. In this case, if you can, please do then go down the slide! It is equally important to let your child see that you coped with an anxious situation. Children need to know that anxiety can be managed.

Scenarios of your own life can be very similar to scenarios of your child's life too. For example, it is common for children in primary school to feel some anxiety the first time they have to recite lines in a school play or stand up in front of the class and present something, prepare for a big spelling test or independently go on a school trip / sleepover for the first time. These are all topics that you can identify with; for example, you may be anxious about a big work presentation or a very important party you have to attend, which can be helpful for your child to hear about. It can resonate with them how they feel at times.

Children also love hearing stories about when mum / dad were little. Sharing times that you felt worried or anxious in your childhood, can also have a positive impact on a child. *'Mum / dad managed that when they were little, so can I!'*

After-effects of anxiety

What is just as important as educating a child about anxiety, is exploring with your child the after-effects of completing or managing something that they felt anxious about. For example, how did they feel after they stood up and said their lines beautifully in assembly or after their first successful sleepover or participated in an enjoyable school trip? Were they proud? Did they want to do it again?

Anxiety can feel scary, especially for a young child, but the more they experience anxiety, the more they will also be able to experience (hopefully) some positive after-effects of it too. The feeling of conquering that worry and anxiety can be immense and hugely satisfying, but children need help to develop this association. Talk to your child about the feelings they had afterwards, demonstrate how proud you are, encourage them to feel that same pride in themselves and remind them of this on other occasions.

It is natural that after participating in something that initially made them feel anxious, your child may subsequently feel tired, or drained. Ensure they have a drink available before and after. There are lots of links between panic and dehydration and sometimes a drink or small snack can help their body regain balance again. It is also important to consider where or what they are going to be doing next. Their mind and body may just need time to relax on the sofa and do nothing, rather than rushing to another activity and not allowing their anxiety levels to settle. Bringing their body back down to a balanced state after experiencing anxiety, is hugely important for overall mental health.

Sadly, there will be occasions when a child is anxious about something and the result is not positive. Maybe they were so anxious, they forgot all their lines in the school play and came out feeling really low. On these occasions, it is easy for negative thought patterns to develop -'every time I feel anxious I will not do well' - so it is important to continue to make sure your child has opportunities to try again and not shy away from these situations. In these cases, lots of reassurance from parents about the process / effort is needed, rather than dwelling on the results of the experience they just had. Focus on how well they did to stand up there despite being so nervous, how brave they were and how hard they worked learning the lines etc.

Opportunities to share their worries and anxieties

Ensure you are providing space and opportunities for your child to share their worries with you. Talking about worries and anxieties can be astronomical in helping to reduce them. It may feel like you are not offering your child much guidance and support by *just listening*, but sometimes all a child needs is a listening ear. A chance to offload and be fully understood, having that space to verbalise out loud how they feel, or think, can often provide opportunities for them to develop their own thought processes and ideas. Sometimes also just sharing a worry, and not seeing the other person shocked or panicked about it, can be Therapeutic in itself - perhaps it is not so bad then, if mum / dad are remaining calm and collected.

All the ideas from our previous 'Encouraging Open Communication' chapter will come into play here, regarding the ways in which you can offer your child opportunities to share their worries and anxieties with you, while remaining calm and managing your own responses. Remember, as discussed, never belittle any form of worry or anxiety, no matter how small it may seem to you as an adult.

Managing the anxiety

Over time, children who understand anxiety and bodily feelings are often able to manage quite well, however, may still need some 'coping skills' too. It is important to remember that with worries and anxieties, some children will just simply want a space to be listened to, while others will be eager to learn 'techniques' and 'strategies' to help them. Each child is unique and must be supported accordingly.

For those looking for more practical ideas, here are a few techniques that can be adapted to suit different ages.

First, I would suggest going through the techniques and learning them yourself, so your own 'toolbox' feels full. This means you can pull out the right 'tool', as and when your child needs it. For some children, if they feel they are learning / being taught something, as they would be in school, they may actively disengage straight away. Instead, try to initiate it as an activity, almost like a fun game. Try to do so in a natural way and in a natural scenario; for example, as you are walking along together, driving in the car, before bed etc. The less staged it feels, the more likely your child is to engage with it.

You can then monitor what your child seems to relate well to and what they do not enjoy. What works for one child, may differ for another and the same goes for siblings too. Once you see your child engage positively with one or two of the techniques, try them out a few times, before explaining to your child, in an appropriate situation, that this game can also be useful when they are feeling a little nervous, or anxious. You can then advise your child on times they may be able to independently use the idea (age dependent).

Ideally your child will be slightly accustomed to the 'technique' (game) so it will be easier for them to use when in a heightened state of anxiety.

Older primary school children may then feel comfortable using the technique, for example, when sitting in class waiting for a test to start. Bear in mind, for this to happen you will probably have to do the techniques with them several times, before they develop skills to independently use them at appropriate times.

Younger children, in early primary school, will generally need the support from an adult to use them, however it is always worth sharing something that really works for your child with their teacher too. If they are one day feeling very anxious at school, the teacher could carry out the activity with your child.

Grounding techniques

The overall aim of these techniques is to encourage a child to focus on the *present* situation. Often anxieties tend to involve many future 'what if' worries, so concentrating on the here and now, can help 'ground' a child to the moment, supporting them to feel calmer.

Anxiety can also feed on itself. If your child has to wait all day at school for a test, or you have a 15-minute walk from the car to the new club they are trying out, anxiety can build and build and feel overwhelming as the wait goes on. A child who is in a very high state of anxiety will find it harder to come down from it, meaning they may not focus as well, or perform to the best of their ability. These 'Grounding Techniques' can stop anxiety escalating to this extent, helping children remain in a more relaxed and calm state.

The 5, 4, 3, 2, 1

This idea can be used anywhere, but I have found it can be useful on the walk to school, if a child is anxious about the day ahead.

Name 5 things you can see

Name 4 things you can feel

Name 3 things you can hear

Name 2 things you can smell

Name 1 thing you can taste

This technique is about fine tuning the senses and focusing on things that we probably often take for granted. Look out for small details, for example, patterns on brick work, light shining off a surface, lines on leaves or funny shapes in the clouds.

It is likely your child may just say 'flower', but on your turn, you can demonstrate more detailed examples - "I see a purple flower, with black dots in the middle, on a long green stem with a green leaf that is slightly turning yellow." Rather than being critical of what your child has noticed, just mirroring ways of looking at objects in a little more detail yourself, can help your child examine items in even greater depth, which can further 'ground' them to the moment.

In terms of things that can be 'felt', explore the feel of clothing, the sensation of the ground against your shoe, the sun shining in your eyes, or the wind blowing your hair etc. You may even like to pick up something, for example a pebble on the ground and share how smooth or rough it may feel.

The 'sound' aspect of this task allows for some moments of calm and quiet, taking in your surroundings - birds, planes, trees, ticking clocks, people...

When exploring the 'smells', this may take a little more concentration. Perhaps there is an air freshener in the room, or maybe freshly cut grass, if you are outside. Maybe you are walking past a bakery and can smell bread baking? Perhaps there are no smells, and maybe you will need to find some - a flower or an unlit candle if you are at home.

In terms of 'taste', perhaps your child can still taste their breakfast, or their toothpaste! This step is a little harder and sometimes offering your child a tiny sweet or small snack for this one can help. Focus attention on the flavour - what does it taste like? Do they like it? Chew it slowly and explore the texture.

The rainbow

List as many things as possible around you which are:

Red, Orange, Yellow, Green, Blue, Indigo, Violet

Try to not only list *one* of each colour - keep going until there is nothing else you can spot, then move on.

Mental exercises

Mental exercises are useful as they can be used anywhere and can take the mind away from anxious thoughts and uncomfortable feelings. The great thing about these, is that for older children they can be carried out in their head, so if in a social or public setting, no one would even know.

Younger children would probably need you to play with them. Again, try out and experiment what works best for your child.

· Name all the objects that you can see around you

· Name all the objects you can see that begin with the same letter of your name

· Count backwards from 100

· Count backwards from 100 by 6 each time

· Recite the alphabet backwards

· Spell out your name and the name of your best friend, backwards

· Pick an object you can see and describe 10 points about it - the colour / texture / size etc.

· List all your family members, then state their favourite colour or favourite thing to do

· ‘Draw’ something just using your mind (or in the air with your finger if appropriate). Imagine drawing an animal or a vehicle and visualise all the lines and details it needs. Colour it in with your mind using an imaginary paint set

Categories

Suggest a random category to your child and ask them to think of as many items as they can in each one. For example, types of cereal, fruit, makes of cars, TV shows, pop singers, books, toys, things to play in the garden etc.

For a further idea, pick a category and try and see if your child can find something in that same category going through all the letters of the alphabet.

Body exercises - Progressive Muscle Relaxation

No need to share the name of it with younger children - just simply, it is their relaxing time!

This idea can be helpful before bed - a time when lots of children may feel particularly worried. It can be useful to get into the habit of adding this to your bedtime routine, if your child is someone who may worry or feel stressed.

It involves tensing (you can call it squeezing to children) and then relaxing all muscles, which brings about a feeling of initial focus and then relaxation.

If practised regularly at home, in time older children may be able to use this technique when sitting in class and feeling anxious.

Sit or lie in a comfortable position and for all the points listed next, encourage your child to pay close attention to how each move feels. Perhaps initially do it with them, lying next to them on their bed for the first few times. Notice how you feel too - it might be something you decide to use yourself in anxious adult situations.

· Curl your toes for 10-seconds then relax them

· Flex your feet for 10-seconds then relax them

· Squeeze your thighs together for 10-seconds, then relax them

· Suck in your tummy for 10-seconds, then let it fully relax

· Squeeze your shoulder blades together for 10-seconds then relax

· Lift your shoulders to your ears for 10-seconds then relax

· Squeeze your fingers into a fist for 10-seconds then relax

· Scrunch your face up for 10-seconds then relax

· Squeeze and tense all the muscles in your body for 10-seconds, then release all tension and relax

Breathing exercises

Breathing exercises can be useful, although do not always interest, or work for everyone. The idea behind them is that deep breathing sends messages to the brain to calm and relax us, which can alleviate symptoms of anxiety, if used in the right way.

Often just telling a child to 'breathe' is not quite enough - they probably think they are breathing anyway, so it can be confusing! Young children also do not instinctively know how to 'deep breathe', so teaching them with props initially can help.

Bubbles

The use of a bubble set encourages slow and careful breathing in order to make the bubbles. After your child has mastered this with the actual prop, in an anxious situation you could suggest to them to imagine they are 'bubble breathing', taking a big breath in and then slowly blowing up their bubbles.

Toys

Place a light toy, like a small stuffed animal on your child's tummy when they are lying down. Encourage them to breathe in and out deeply, causing the stuffed animal on their tummy to move up and down, so they can visually see it - a bit like taking their animal on a fairground ride! This teaches children deep tummy breathing and later you can encourage them to use their 'animal breathing' when in anxious situations.

For slightly older children the 5, 2, 6 number approach can be helpful and easy to remember.

Breathe in for 5, hold for 2, breathe out for 6, counting in your head as you do each step. Do this with your child the first few times and they may then be able to use this idea in situations, on their own.

In terms of all the ideas and different techniques, please remember, do not teach your child *all* these concepts, as that would be overwhelming, and they would get no benefit from them.

Introduce ideas naturally and slowly over time, in a fun way and see what works for your child.

Rational and irrational thoughts

For older children in primary school, teach your child the words 'Rational' and 'Irrational' and how this can be applied to our thoughts. Help them understand that everyone, including adults, experience rational and irrational thinking processes.

For much younger children in primary school, perhaps think of names (instead of irrational and rational) that your child could relate to. If they think of a certain animal as funny or a bit silly, you could use this. For example, an irrational thought could be called 'a monkey thought' and let them then make up their own name for a rational thought - perhaps they may just like to call it an 'OK thought'.

'I am going to be late for school and may get in trouble' - this is likely to be a rational thought.

'I am going to be late for school and get in trouble and all my friends will hate me and I will not be invited to anyone's party anymore and then I will get expelled from school and have no friends forever' - this is likely to be an opposing irrational thought.

Quite simply, an irrational thought is something that is unrealistic - these thoughts are natural but can be highly annoying and frustrating. They can also make anxiety feel magnified.

A rational thought is something that tends to be based on fact. For example, 'I am going to be late for school' (fact: it is already 8.10am) and 'I may get into trouble' (fact: the teacher was angry when Charles arrived late yesterday).

If you see your child experiencing irrational thoughts, the following questions can be useful to consider with them.

Is that a monkey thought or an OK thought? (Use the real words for older children)

Is that thought a fact or feeling?

What would .... (their best friend) think about this situation?

How *likely* is it that it will actually come true? (for older children they could give a percentage out of one hundred - generally low percentages, should help alleviate some of the 'power' of the thought)

What is actually likely to happen?

Thoughts have the power to change how anyone feels - if we think of something sad, we are likely to feel sad and vice-versa. Identifying and taming irrational, unhelpful thoughts is an important 'tool' to learn.

When anxiety is escalating further

So far, all the previous points mainly focus on general, everyday anxiety and how to stop it escalating to a point that it starts to become debilitating.

There is a point when general anxieties can increase and start to influence your child's everyday life, but perhaps not to the extent that it may be causing great stress and not what I would consider to be anywhere near a diagnosable anxiety disorder. This could be due to factors such as, general worldly events, peer relationships, bullying, excess stress over homework, exams, anxieties over changes at home, marital breakdowns or moving schools etc.

The following ideas are useful to consider, not just for everyday anxiety and worry, but also for when it is escalating slightly beyond this point.

Massage

As an adult, I am sure many of us enjoy a massage, or a spa day as special treat and the same goes for children too. 'Baby Massage' is hugely popular for newborns, in assisting with all sorts of common ailments, but can be very helpful for children of primary school age too. Massage releases a hormone called oxytocin which helps us to feel relaxed. A 10-minute back rub before your child goes to sleep may help to relax them if they are particularly worried. This may encourage them to sleep better, helping your child 'cope' more rationally with the worry, the following day.

Resources

The use of sensory items, like slime, putty, kinetic sand, playdough and clay, mentioned in our 'Encouraging Open Communications' chapter are also really useful for children with anxiety. The physical sensation of playing with these items can help release tension and stress.

It is common to think of 'fidget toys' as items that are commonly used for children with diagnosable conditions like ADHD (Attention Deficit Hyperactivity Disorder) and autism, however they can be just as useful for children who may be anxious at times. Try finding something very small that your child can keep in their pocket that they can fidget with, if need be.

Colouring can be hugely relaxing, with lots of thinking suggesting the repetitive motion of it activates certain brain pathways, allowing refocus and anxiety reduction. I have found 'adult colouring books' to be really helpful for children of primary school age, and more useful than just giving a child a blank piece of paper and suggesting they colour.

Other activities like colour by numbers, or LEGO® sets, as well as the ideas listed in our 'Quiet Time Box' from our 'Developing Positive Sleep Patterns' chapter are all calming and can stop negative thoughts escalating, refocusing the mind.

Worry box / worry monster

'Worry Monsters' can be purchased online, or alternatively, if you are feeling inventive you could make one yourself. The idea is that children write down or draw a worry and put it in the monster's mouth and she / he gobbles it up. (Mum / dad take out the worry an hour later).

This can be helpful for mild worries as a way of releasing the fret from your child's mind.

For a child who may not like the idea of a 'monster', or for slightly older children, you could have a 'worry box' in your home whereby children can write down any worries they may have and post them inside. At the end of the day, or week, mum / dad goes through the 'post' in the worry box and talks it through with their child. You may find some worries have gone - just the notion of writing it down and getting it out their head can help - or other worries may still be present that can be discussed together.

Naming the worry

Sometimes naming the worry can be helpful for children. When they feel anxious you can say something along the lines of "Oh is Mr / Mrs Worry Bug back again? What is Worry Bug saying today? What is he / she making you feel?"

You can then think of ways to 'defeat' Mr / Mrs Worry Bug!

You can choose a name together - just make sure it is non-human related.

Naming a general worry can lessen the fear a little. It can also help a younger child who may be experiencing a confusing worried or anxious feeling, but cannot quite name what it is or why.

Therapeutic stories

If your child has experienced something specific which has made them anxious, it is always worth researching 'Therapeutic Stories'. These are books, relating to common aspects of childhood, that focus on a character who has experienced something similar. This non-direct style of writing can resonate with many children. They can 'recognise' a particular worry associated with the character in the story. By focusing only on the character, and *their* experience, helps a child internally process their own worry / anxiety. It is better not to compare the worry or anxiety to your own child's, as this may feel too difficult for them. If you are wanting to discuss the book with your child, focus on the character and the character's situation and feelings only. Suggesting something along the lines of "that sounds like you and your friend" can be unhelpful and too directive.

External sounds

As mentioned previously, it is customary for many families to have the news on in the mornings, or the radio on in the car. Even in the manic rush of getting ready for school, children will still take in and absorb things they hear. Remember the news is not written for children, therefore the facts will not be age-appropriate. It is common for children to hear things, not fully comprehend what they have heard, and go away and worry about it. In their minds, they turn it round and relate it to themselves or their families; it does not always have to be a catastrophic event either. Unrealistic and scary thoughts can grow with the aid of their imagination. Any worldly events you think they should be made aware of, need to come from you as their parents, who are the 'filter', not news channels aimed at adults.

Case Study: Barney aged 5

Barney had general anxieties that were beginning to impact on his behaviour. His parents noticed he would often avoid certain activities or places and they were unsure why. In his Therapy sessions Barney would frequently play 'tsunamis' in the sand. He would cover the small world toys he was engaging with, explaining that the people were 'drowning.'

It turns out this topic was never covered at home, or at school, and in fact Barney had inadvertently seen news images on TV of a recent tsunami abroad, causing him to become scared of water, bath time and the beach. Barney's family were oblivious of the fact that he had seen this, and therefore unaware he needed reassurance or guidance that he was safe. Instead, Barney was trying to cope with having seen explicit and scary images of water from TV, having no understanding of what it meant.

Monitoring your child's play

We have mentioned how sometimes just being able to talk and offload their worries is all a child needs, however for a very young primary school child, like Barney, it is probable that they cannot verbalise or understand their worries. This is where the importance of play comes in. We discussed in our 'Schedules, Clubs and Free-Time' chapter the importance of children having this unstructured time and free-play, not only to help them relax, but also to help them understand and express their inner world. For young children, play is their natural language. You cannot expect them to sit down and have an adult conversation about their anxieties, but they *will* demonstrate their thoughts in their play. Had Barney not played out his thoughts regarding tsunamis, we possibly would never have fully understood this internal anxiety he was experiencing. This is exactly how Therapy for a very young child in primary school works - we explore and understand their inner world through the toys.

I am not suggesting that as parents, you need to act as your child's Therapist - children need you as their mum / dad, not their Therapist, but you can increase your awareness around your child's play. It will help you become a little more mindful of what they may be unconsciously feeling and experiencing, and any anxieties that may be giving them concern.

Here are some ideas of how to do this...

· When you play with your child, try to keep 'one foot in the play and one foot out', (get involved and have fun - after all no one wants to play with someone who is not exciting and engaging with the characters), but remain aware of what is happening. It can be easy to get swept up in a child's play, or role play, and miss certain things they are expressing.

· Notice themes if you can. Often play can be about friendship dynamics, which can help you understand your child's inner world a little more in terms of situations with their peers.

· Notice what you see - "hmmm that elephant seems a bit upset right now."

· Try to have two voices - one for the character of the elephant and one that sounds like mum / dad when you are slightly stepping out of the play and reflecting on what you can see happening. A *reflection* would be something along the lines of our elephant comment in the latter point.

· Saying that, do not reflect too much - keep a balance between engaging in the play as the character, and occasionally adding in a reflective comment as mum / dad.

· Do not deviate from the character - if your child is playing out a story, do not say, "oh that is exactly like you and your sister!" - stick to the *character's* feelings. If a child is choosing to use other figures, not themselves in the play, it is because this is what they *need* to do, as being too direct can sometimes feel scary.

· Do not worry about certain aspects of your child's play - even if some situations do sometimes seem scary, or unkind, this is your child's way of sorting out the very confusing thoughts and emotions in their head - children process this through play. Of course, if any of their play concerns you greatly, then do seek advice.

Let us explore the importance of play a little further with the example of Matthew.

Case Study: Matthew aged 7

Matthew had experienced multiple operations before his third birthday, due to a congenital heart condition. Every single session, during Therapy, Matthew would play 'doctors'. He would take turns in being the patient and the doctor, fixing a range of ailments, always including a specific focus on the stethoscope. He would check how fast the heart was beating and if it was 'working.' This play, alongside an understanding adult who could reflect with

Matthew on his actions, was highly Therapeutic. This is how Matthew processed what had happened to him and anxieties about doctors in general, by playing out medical scenarios repeatedly. In time, Matthew moved on, away from 'doctors' - he had processed what he needed.

As parents, never underestimate the importance and power of play!

Tummy pain

It is incredibly common for children to experience tummy pain as a result of anxiety (although this must be investigated by a doctor to ensure it is not medical). This feeling of unexplained soreness can be frightening for children of primary school age who may think they are unwell. I am sure there are many parents who have kept their child off school because they thought they had a tummy bug developing, which miraculously disappeared after a relaxing day at home. Often this is not children making up an excuse to stay home, but a physical pain that they do feel. It may be an idea to explain to your child that sometimes people can experience tummy pains when they feel anxious or nervous.

Try to keep a diary of when your child complains about their tummy - is it before a routine event, or after? Is it school related? Home related? Person related? Is your child fine on weekends? Identifying the trigger can be hugely helpful. You may need help from the teacher to also track episodes of tummy pain at school. Perhaps you notice that it is always on a Wednesday... the teacher then notices, for example, if it is always before PE.

If you do notice a pattern, it is then easier to manage and help the situation. It is likely that a primary school child cannot independently notice these associations, so they will need help from mum / dad.

Do remember, a child who is suffering from severe levels of anxiety, especially over a prolonged period, may require external help to get to the root of the problem and manage the effects. The following and final chapter will now discuss the alternative avenues one can go down, if you have ongoing concerns relating to your child's mental health.

Key 'takeaways' from this chapter to support positive mental health:

✓ As parents, it is possible for you to take steps and strive to prevent heightened anxiety (through consistency, boundaries, appropriate routines, open communication, encouraging emotional expression and supporting emotional education)

- ✓ Consider the importance of educating your child on the difference between worry and anxiety and how it is acceptable and healthy to experience these mildly throughout the week

- ✓ Consider educating your child on the positive and negative after-effects of anxiety

- ✓ Consider sharing with your child some of your own worries and anxieties (in age-appropriate ways) and the bodily sensations that accompany them

- ✓ Ensure there are opportunities for your child to share worries and anxieties and monitor your own response

- ✓ For younger children, observe play, and anxieties that may surface in their play

- ✓ Learn the 'tools' and techniques that can be used to help everyday anxiety, as well as heightened anxiety and over time share these with your child

- ✓ Consider when to seek help for anxiety that is beyond appropriate levels

CHAPTER TWELVE

The Route to Therapeutic Support

When to seek help and how to start?

Although the chapters in this book discuss ways that you can achieve key Therapeutic goals around positive mental health at home, there are however, always going to be some occasions when professional help may still be required. There might, at times, be extremely difficult childhood experiences or encounters and aspects of a child's life that parents cannot control. This may mean it is necessary to seek some extra support - it is nothing to be ashamed of - if our child were sick or had a broken bone, we would seek support. This is no different.

Accessing Therapy for children can be confusing and at times difficult. I have observed that sometimes this can discourage parents as it is not always quite as simple as going into the pharmacy for some extra Vitamin C tablets.

I hope however, that the next few paragraphs will lay out as clearly as possible, the different routes that you can take, in order to ensure you can access appropriate support for your child. Whether you have read this book and have decided to access support now, or return to this chapter in a year, the following guidance is aimed at offering a helping hand in the subsequent steps you need to take. I have read so many online articles, or books, which simply reference parents to *'seek support from a professional'*, but I personally feel this is not always helpful, if a parent does not know *how* to go about seeking this support.

It can sometimes be difficult to tell the difference between general challenging behaviours, in line with child development, or something that is deemed a cause for concern. In general, if your concerns or your child's behaviour persists over many weeks, or longer, and amendments at home are not making any difference, it may be time to look into seeking some help. A further indicator that extra support may be necessary, is if behaviours and concerns are beginning to interfere with school and overall functioning and your child's personality or temperament seems to be changing. If a child's behaviour is unsafe, or your child shares wanting to harm themselves, or someone else or demonstrating severe anxiety, then always seek help *straight away.* I would strongly recommend beginning the process of accessing support, sooner rather than later. Many families come to me after years of struggling. They either did not know how to access support, hoped things would improve, or saw intermittent glimmers of hope so they felt it may not be necessary. Of course, all of these thought processes make complete sense, but from a Therapeutic perspective, a child who has been struggling for years, may require much more long-term support as many of their thoughts and behavioural patterns are likely to have become quite ingrained. In comparison, a child who has only been having difficulties for a few months, may only need brief, short-term intervention.

As with anything health related, or learning related, early intervention is imperative - the sooner we access help the better - and often the easier it is then to bring about positive change.

As mentioned, it is important to associate mental health in the same way as other aspects of our health, despite it being harder to physically 'see'. It can help our mindset to feel more confident in pursuing help, if we view it in the same way as making an appointment with a doctor for a medical issue.

For example, if your child had potentially fractured their leg, you would almost definitely seek support quickly, rushing straight to the Accident and Emergency Department. The sooner you sought this help, hopefully the quicker your child would be on the mend. However, if you wait, hoping it is not serious and that it will improve by itself, the likelihood is that more damage may be caused. By the time you seek help, perhaps the fracture and surrounding tissue has been effected, so the healing process may take longer now. Perhaps the bone has also aggravated the muscle a little, so now your child needs support with not just the fracture, but the muscle as well. What about if you wait, or never seek help for it - your child will learn ways to walk and manage with the fracture every day and soon it becomes a way of life that they have accepted. It makes every day difficult, but you and your child learn and alter your behaviour to cope with it - potentially this may make the healing process a lot more complex than if earlier help had been sought.

It is important that mental health needs are viewed in the same way.

One question every parent understandably asks me, is "how many sessions will my child need?" As frustrating as it is for families, I can never answer this, as I simply do not know how a child will respond to Therapy. On average, I have seen great improvements for some children after just six sessions, whereas with others it is common for me to work with them for many months, and some for at least a year, if not two. To see a positive change, be ready to accept that it will generally take several months, but of course this is highly dependent on your child, the Therapist / their experience, and the reason for seeking support. When a child begins Therapy, the Therapist to them is a stranger, so it takes time for a feeling of trust and security to develop. Therapy involves revealing highly personal aspects of oneself to another person, whether that be directly through talking, or indirectly through playing. In order to enable this to happen and for changes to ensue, the child needs to develop a positive relationship with their Therapist, which can take time.

The different routes of accessing Therapy

If you are concerned about your child and feel strongly that they may benefit from some external professional support, there are three main routes that you could investigate. I will explore some advantages and disadvantages of each different route, so you can decide what you feel would work best for your child and your family. Bear in mind, due to the shortage of mental health services, there may not be a choice with regards to the route that you go down. This guidance is based on my own experience over the years, but of course may differ depending on your location.

Primary school mental health services

Your child's school is probably the first port of call, as many schools nowadays do have a mental health professional working with them who can offer Therapy sessions. Like all services, some schools have waiting lists for these facilities so it is important to find out when the school expects they would be able to offer help.

Some schools offer mental health support groups in the interim, whereby several children come together in a small group once a week and participate in sessions together - topics are often based around friendships and feelings and emotions. Although this would not be classed as Therapy, groups of this kind can be very beneficial, whilst waiting for a one-to-one place to open up. Ask your school about this and see what they can offer.

If your child is offered a place within a school Counselling / Therapy service, your child would attend this during school hours, usually once a week and usually at the same time and on the same day each week, giving them consistency.

Potential advantages of school-based services

- If your child enjoys school, it is likely they will be comfortable within the school environment, so it may help them feel more at ease settling into their Therapy sessions, which are provided on the school site

- They may have seen other children accessing this support, or even their close friends, which can 'normalise' Therapy, helping children to engage and feel more comfortable attending

- They may have seen the Therapist around the school or observed him or her provide class talks. Children are therefore already aware of who the individual is, which can be comforting

- It is free for parents to access

- Practically, it may be easier for parents as you do not need to take your child to an external appointment each week

- The Therapist may also offer insight or strategies that your child's teacher can put in place, meaning your child has access to a wider support network

Potential disadvantages of school-based services

- Not all schools offer this service

- It may be time limited if schools have a high demand, so they may only offer a certain number of sessions per child

- If concerns relate to school or peers, your child may find it difficult to open up about this, when sessions are provided within the school environment

- Some children may find it difficult knowing their peers are aware of their sessions and may want more privacy

- Unless their session is at lunchtime, children are likely to miss an academic lesson each week

- Some children may find it difficult, if they have had a troubling session, to return to lessons straight after, finding the transition challenging

- If schools have no concerns about how the child is coping during the school day, it may be harder to access this support, if the concerns are more related to behaviours at home

- Sessions are not run during school holidays. These breaks can cause difficulties for *some* children who rely on the support, meaning that sometimes sessions can lack consistency, especially during the long summer break

- Some schools work as a placement service, so the Therapist your child sees may be in-training, or not fully qualified

NHS mental health services

If your child's school does not provide a Therapeutic service, or if you feel more comfortable seeking this support away from school, your next option would likely be to arrange an appointment with your child's GP.

It may be helpful to arrange the appointment by yourself first, so you can openly talk through your concerns, without your child being present. Your GP will probably then decide if they would like to see your child in person, at a follow-up appointment.

It is important to note that GPs are *not* mental health professionals, so your child will not be accessing Therapy with them. If they are not too concerned by what you are sharing, they may give you some basic advice themselves. On the other hand, they may point you in the direction of another professional that they feel could be better suited to help or they may agree to an NHS referral to Child and Adolescent Mental Health Services. From my experience, it appears every GP works in slightly different ways, however, you are well within your right to push for a referral, if this is the route you would like to take.

It is necessary to realise that if your child is referred for NHS mental health support, the waiting list for this could be very long. It is also important to be aware that your child may not even receive support this way, if they are not deemed to reach certain risk thresholds. The mental health team in the NHS are highly trained Therapists, Doctors, Psychologists and Psychiatrists and offer fantastic services to support children. Unfortunately, they are just completely overstretched, given the numbers of children in need of this support. Please consider that although they do work with a wide variety of difficulties, many of the children and young people they see are in severe need, in terms of presenting with eating disorders, self-harm behaviours, suicidal attempts, and overdoses. They therefore must prioritise who they see and when, in terms of immediate need. If you are requesting a referral because of a mild friendship difficulty which you feel is affecting your child's mental health, you may be waiting some time for support.

Of course, things change all the time in terms of government funding allowances, but at the time of publishing, I have seen first-hand many clients waiting well over a year for NHS support. For those trying to access assessments, in terms of autism or ADHD (Attention Deficit Hyperactivity Disorder), I have had clients waiting over two years. This will differ depending on your location or borough.

Potential advantages of NHS support

· Your child may have access to a range of different child specialists, who can tailor Therapy to their exact need

· The service is free of charge to parents

· Children access this externally, away from school, which may make some feel more comfortable, allowing more privacy from peers

· All services are for children and young people, so the service should feel child friendly

· You may be offered Parent Therapy and / or Parent Support at the same time, complimenting your child's Therapy

· If the Therapist has any further concerns, they may be able to quickly refer your child to another team member, who may be specialised in that field

Potential disadvantages of NHS support

· The waiting lists can be incredibly long

· There is a chance that your child may not even be able to access support, depending on thresholds

· Therapy can be time limited; I have known some children only be offered 6 sessions, which is sometimes not enough

· Some children may feel anxious about having to attend an external, unfamiliar setting

· There may not be much flexibility in appointment times, so you may have to take your child out of school each week and change your own schedule to fit around what is offered

· Practically, it may be harder for working parents, or those with other children to attend appointments each week, if the service is not too close to home

Private mental health services

Often people access private support if they have not had much luck from the school, GP or NHS mental health team, or if they are very keen to begin Therapy as soon as possible. Going down this route, your child could begin Therapy, depending on the demand of your chosen Therapist, potentially within a week.

I would always suggest to anyone seeking private support, to still request a referral for NHS Therapy, just so that your child is in the system and on their waiting list. You may need to use this further down the line. Parents can always turn down this offer, if and when an NHS place becomes available. Should your finances change dramatically and you are unable to afford to continue privately, or circumstances change for the Therapist, it is good to still have the back-up of the NHS option. If your child is progressing well with the private Therapist and you are able to continue, it is however always advisable to stay with the same Therapist.

When looking for a private Therapist, it is best to find someone who specialises in children. Many Therapists who work with adults, offer additional sessions for children, but it is important to look at their qualifications and ensure that they have had specific training in this area. Working with adults is very different to working with children.

Worryingly so, at the time of publishing, there is little regulation for Therapists - anybody can do an online course and then say they are a 'Therapist' which can be incredibly confusing. There is work being done to rectify this and make the regulations clearer, as it is very concerning that someone could be seeking support from a professional who does not have the appropriate skills and who has completed some very basic training in a matter of days / weeks.

As well as checking that the Therapist is qualified to work with children, ensure that they are regulated with an Awarding Body. To be allowed to register with an Awarding Body, a professional Therapist goes through a robust procedure whereby their qualifications are certified, and certain requirements must be met. Only Therapists who have officially trained for years can become associated with an Awarding Body.

The Awarding Bodies to look out for may include:

BACP - British Association of Counselling and Psychotherapy

BPS - British Psychological Society

BAPT - British Association of Play Therapists

Asking the school, your friends, your GP, or local children's services for names of reputable private Child Therapists is a good idea. It is always helpful to have a personal recommendation.

Private Therapists tend to work from a room within their home, an outbuilding in their garden, hired rooms in children's centres / GP offices or hired rooms in commercial, shared offices. When choosing your child's Therapist, you can also consider where your child may feel most comfortable attending.

Potential advantages of private Therapy

· Support can usually be accessed very quickly, preventing further mental health decline

· Sessions are not time limited, and your child can attend for as long as you feel the need - the Therapist is not under pressure to meet certain goals within a few short sessions

· Some Therapists may be registered to take insurance, so if you have private medical care, you may be able to access this for free. Many Therapists offer concessional rates to those on lower incomes

· The sessions are external from school, so a child may feel more comfortable attending, away from peers

· Sessions are usually run after school, so no academic lessons are missed

· Depending on the Therapist's availability, you will have more say on the day and time of the session, to suit your family's schedule

· You get a choice of who your child sees and you can speak with a few different Therapists to ensure you find someone you feel comfortable with

Potential disadvantages of private Therapy

· Parents pay for this support and for long-term work this can become costly. Average session prices vary so much, depending on where you live and the experience of the Therapist, but you would probably be looking, at the time of publishing, of paying anything between £40 to £150 a session; more likely the lower end of the scale for a primary school aged child (£40 - £80).

· Private Therapists usually work alone, so if your child needed additional, specialised help alongside their Therapy, you may need to find this support elsewhere yourself

· You would need to take your child to their appointment and collect them each week, which can be hard with busy schedules

· When family finances are involved it can put pressure on all, and pressure on the child to 'feel better' if they are aware of the costs involved

If possible, try not to discuss with your child anything finance related, in terms of their sessions.

Further options

If private Therapy is not an option, the school is offering no assistance and the NHS have a long waiting list, then whilst striving to support your child at home, the following options could be considered:

- Depending on where you live, it may be useful to research youth counselling centres, or youth support services. They may have a waiting list, but it is still always worth looking into these.

- Ask if your child could meet with the school SENCO once a week, for a quick drop-in chat. They may not be a mental health trained professional, but they will be experienced in managing the emotional needs of children to some extent. It may help your child to speak to someone who is not a family member or teacher once a week. Of course, this would not be classed as Therapy, but more of a way of receiving extra support.

- Suggest if the school can offer your child a 'time-out' space, so if they are struggling or feeling emotionally overwhelmed, there is somewhere safe for them to go, for example a quiet room or library.

- Look into other specific clubs which may be more financially manageable. For example, LEGO® Therapy sessions can help with self-esteem, friendship difficulties, confidence, and anxiety.

- Research 'workshops' in your area that your child could attend. There are many companies that provide 'confidence boosting' or 'resilience' workshops which run during the school holidays or after school. These can offer children extra coping strategies, and again are of a much lower cost than regular Therapy.

- If developmentally appropriate, teach your child how to access free services, such as Childline. I think sometimes there can be a stigma associated with services related to the NSPCC, in that they are only for children who may be abused or neglected. Having worked in the past for this service myself, I can assure you much of the time, it is children in late primary school just wanting to phone for a chat because a friend may have been unkind, or because they were upset about moving house or school etc. Any child is welcome to chat to the trained Childline counsellors, and sometimes it can be a weight lifted off their shoulders just to offload onto someone external, who is not mum or dad. Educating your child about these services, demonstrates your acceptance of them. At the time of publishing, Childline also have an online chat service where children can type to a trained counsellor, if they feel this is easier than talking on the phone. You could always set this up for your child, leave the room and let them chat. Both the phone and the online chat services are completely free of charge.

- Research if there are any one-off parenting talks or workshops, relating to childhood mental health that *you* could attend, or ask the school if they know of any companies who run these. Again, there may be a fee to attend, but it could equip you with even more skills to help support your child, if Therapy is not accessible.

- Find out if there are any private Therapists offering much lower, concessional rates. Many Therapists will offer this, particularly if you take your child out during the school day filling one of their slots, which is not so popular. Although I can completely understand not wanting to take a child out of school, and I am not an advocate of a child missing school, it is important to consider that poor mental health in the long run, can negatively affect overall academic attainment. For a short period of time, missing a lesson once a week, for some children, can be more beneficial than detrimental. If you find a private Therapist whom you like the sound of, do not be afraid to ask them if they would work this way, even if they actively do not advertise it.

- Talk to your local council to see if there are any funded support workshops, external from school, that your child may be able to attend in the evenings or on weekends. Sometimes Children's Centres or certain businesses may provide these free services, so it is always worth looking into this.

It can be difficult to access the right support, at the right time for your child, which is why understandably many people wait and hope difficulties improve on their own. This can happen, but it can also go the other way and become a larger problem.

I sincerely hope you will find this book helpful in supporting the well-being of your child. We all, as human beings, can develop mental health issues, but by implementing some of the ideas in these chapters, it may be possible for you to steer your child away from pit-falls that could grow into craters. Let us all, as parents, talk openly and honestly, without embarrassment or shame about issues our children may be going through. Please share this book with friends and family so we can all take steps towards keeping our children happy, relaxed, positive, and confident little people!

If you would like to get in touch with me, please email tammy@counsellingforchildren.org.uk although please bear in mind that without meeting your child, I cannot provide individual advice.

References

The websites listed have been referenced within this book and may be useful for your perusal:

www.place2be.org.uk

www.gosh.nhs.uk

www.nhs.uk

www.childline.co.uk

www.gov.uk

Acknowledgements

This book could not have been written without the amazing and thought-provoking experiences I have encountered, through working with so many incredible children and young people who have come through my doors for Therapy sessions. I would like to thank every single one of them, all of whom have been so courageous to share their inner world and thoughts with me and I feel very privileged to have been a part of their journey.

A huge thank you to my family for their patience and support in writing this book and the time and care they took to read through multiple different drafts! Their opinions and insight have been invaluable in helping the book come to life.

Thank you to my husband for giving up the home office, enabling me to write this book and completing all his own work from a small kitchen table!

Finally, the biggest thanks must go to my editor, Pamela Bentley, who has spent a considerable number of hours, days and weeks painstakingly going through each page of the book, checking dozens of drafts, re-reading extracts over and over and providing instrumental feedback, support and encouragement. Deadlines and timings for publication would not have been possible without Pam's positive work ethic and motivation.

Notes

Please use the following pages to jot down your thoughts, answers to questions or points and ideas that you would like to refer back to

Printed in Great Britain
by Amazon

46883488R00180